A BOOK FOR FAMILY READING

BOOK 2

A BOOK FOR FAMILY READING

The cat's birthday

and other stories that teach biblical truths

Jim Cromarty

EVANGELICAL PRESS

EVANGELICAL PRESS
12 Wooler Street, Darlington, Co. Durham, DL1 1RQ, England

First published 1996

British Library Cataloguing in Publication Data available

ISBN 0 85234-352-3

Printed and bound in Great Britain at The Bath Press, Bath

To my brother
John and his wife Elizabeth
whose many valuable suggestions
assisted in the writing of this book.

Contents

Foreword

by John MacArthur Jr

When our children were growing up Patricia and I were constantly looking for good reading for our family times together. Each morning we would gather around the breakfast table and before we all scattered to school, or work, or whatever, we would read together a portion of God's Word and a brief reading from some Christian author.

We went through several editions of *Pilgrim's Progress*, we read samples of various Christian classics, and we tried several volumes designed for family devotions from a number of Christian publishers. We were always on the lookout for things that were interesting and readable and understandable — and above all, stories that taught biblical truths clearly.

How I wish Jim Cromarty's delightful series had been available to us then! Just right for family readings, these stories are simple and understandable enough even for small children. But the spiritual lessons they teach are fitting for Mum and Dad as well.

Christian parents everywhere will eagerly welcome these readings — and hope that there are many more to come from the pen of Mr Cromarty.

Preface

This second book of stories follows the plan of the initial writing. The stories are again based upon incidents in my own life and the lives of those close to me. From these incidents biblical truths are taught. The aim of the writing is to encourage young folk to turn to the Scriptures and by God's grace come to a saving knowledge of Jesus Christ, the Son of God, as their Lord and Saviour.

Once again I stress that great responsibilities rest upon parents to take care of all aspects of life with their children. So much time and money is devoted to ensuring they gain an education that will provide them with a well-paid job and so a degree of security in our troubled world. Yet so many parents devote such a small amount of time, energy and resources to the spiritual well-being of their children.

The following fifty-two stories involve the reading of a scriptural passage and questions that should provide the basis for family discussion of the biblical truths drawn out in the stories. Those using the studies with children should encourage the learning of the biblical text at the commencement of the story. I urge parents to show a real interest in the spiritual growth of their children. Be willing to set aside a regular time each day for spiritual worship and biblical instruction.

There are fifty-two stories in the book in order that on one particular day of each week one story could be used for family worship — thus families have a year's supply of studies. In the preface to Volume 1 I suggested that the stories there could be used each Sunday. Maybe these stories could be 'Monday stories'. Or, used on a daily basis, together with volume 1 of *A book for family reading*, parents have a family worship programme for a period in excess of a quarter of the year.

These stories should be of value to all who are involved in teaching young folk of the glory of our God and salvation through Jesus Christ.

It is my sincere prayer that God, through his Spirit, might use this small book to bring people to faith in Christ.

A reminder to parents

As I wrote in Volume 1, be willing to sit down with your children and talk to them about spiritual issues. Always have an open ear to listen to their problems and joys. Encourage your children by setting them an example of godly living. Always uphold them before the Lord in your prayers.

May God be pleased to bless all who read these stories.

Jim Cromarty
August 1996

STORY 1

The cat's birthday

Read

Matthew 10:1-15

'Do not give what is holy to the dogs; nor cast your pearls before swine, lest they trample them under their feet, and turn and tear you in pieces' (Matthew 7:6).

There are some words in the Bible that are hard to understand. We read about justification and sanctification and most people have no idea what is meant by those words. Then there are passages of Scripture that cause people much concern. The text for today is one of those difficult texts, but I will try to explain it to you.

The things that are holy are all those things concerning God, and the pearl that is spoken about in the text is the wonderful salvation that is found through faith in Jesus Christ, the Son of God. The dogs and pigs are those people who do not value the precious truths of God's Word. They are the people who blaspheme the holy name of Jesus and continually mock the things of God. They are the people who continually ridicule the followers of Jesus.

Well, a story...

Most children have pets and our four daughters were no different to other children. At various times we had a dog, a bird, white mice, too many cats to remember and there was a period when guinea pigs were very popular. Over a twelve-month period we had about sixty guinea pigs — and we only started with two. But the girls kept a family tree and we knew who was related to whom, and each guinea pig had a name. They bred so well that many children at school were given guinea pigs at no cost at all.

But somehow cats were the most popular pets. There always seemed to be a cat or two attached to the family. Every now and again one would be run over by a car and the tears would flow. Then there would be a replacement — and on it went.

Our daughter Cathie had a favourite cat, Sox. Sox was dumped outside our house one night and the next morning there on the doorstep was a half-grown male cat — jet black in colour and with four lovely white feet. Cathie was the first to see the new arrival and at once she came and asked if the cat could come inside. I said that we had enough pets and no one was to take any notice of the cat, hoping that if we ignored it, it would find its way back home.

But that evening the cat was still sitting on the doorstep. So it had to be fed, but I insisted it could not come into the house. Within several days the cat, now called 'Soxie', had become Cathie's special friend. Then as we were sitting around the oil heater Cathie asked, 'Please may I bring Sox into the lounge room where it is warm?'

So the door was opened and in raced Sox. He simply ran to my chair and jumped up onto my lap — turned around several times and was soon purring. Then came the question I dreaded: 'May we keep Soxie as our pet?'

So Sox lived with us for many years. I think he was one of the few cats that died of old age. But Cathie recorded the date of Sox's arrival and each year he had a birthday party. Now in Australia the date of horses' birthday is 1 August, and everyone who has a pet horse makes sure there are some carrots and a few sugar cubes for the horse on that day. I can't remember the date of Sox's birthday, but I remember well before one birthday that Cathie decided Sox would have a new plastic food container and a special treat. She decided that that year she would buy some of the most delicious cat food she could afford. It was going to be a real celebration for Sox. The other family cat had the old dish that was washed every now and again — and he would eat the table scraps. Sox was to have the very best on his birthday.

Well, the time came, the dish was out, the tin of food was opened and the contents put in the dish. The cat food smelled so delicious I think I could have eaten it. But when Sox was given his food, he just took a sniff, turned away and walked over to the old smelly dish containing the scraps from the table and had a feed with the other cat.

Cathie then decided that Sox would not get any special treatment again. He did, however, and he was greatly loved by the girls. When he died and was buried in the back garden with a cross to mark his resting-place, Cathie said that even Mum and Dad had tears in their eyes.

The most wonderful story anyone can know is the story of Christ's salvation. Sinners need a Saviour, and Jesus Christ is the only one who can save sinners. Yet so many, when they hear the gospel story, turn away and go their own way. They are just like Sox, who refused to eat the delicious food and turned away to second best.

But Christians are called to remind these people of their great need of Jesus Christ. Most people simply ignore our witnessing, but there are some who curse using the name of Jesus Christ. They openly mock Christians, the beautiful gospel story and ridicule the person of Jesus Christ.

In our reading for today, Jesus sent the disciples out to preach the good news of the kingdom of God. But he told the disciples that if people would not listen to their words, they were to leave the house where they were speaking and go to someone who would listen. The disciples were told to leave a village where the people mocked their preaching. The gospel is precious, Christ is precious and if people continually blaspheme our God and the gospel, then there comes a time when we should leave that person and take the gospel to others who will pay attention. This sounds hard, but it is what the Scriptures teach. Remember Pharaoh, who saw the power of God's miracles in Egypt. He refused to let God's people leave his country and we read that God hardened Pharaoh's heart so that he could not believe and obey God's commandments (Read Romans 9:17-18).

Friends, don't waste the good news of the gospel. Today is the day to turn to Jesus and believe. Today is the day to ask God's Spirit to change your heart. Today is the day to repent of your sins and live the life of righteousness. Tomorrow may be too late. If you reject the call to faith, God may leave you in your sins. The end is too terrible to think about.

Reader, hell is real and salvation through faith in Christ is also real. If you are not a Christian then ask God to save you.

Activities

1. What is the 'good news' that is found in the Bible?
2. What did Jesus mean by his words: 'Do not give what is holy to dogs; nor cast your pearls before swine...' ? (Matthew 7:6).
3. What is meant by 'blasphemy'?

STORY 2

The training of the Lord

Read

2 Samuel 12:1-15

> My son, do not despise the chastening of the LORD, nor be discouraged when you are rebuked by Him; For whom the LORD loves He chastens, and scourges every son whom He receives' (Hebrews 12:5-6).

Our God is most concerned with the way his people live. All of God's people are called to holiness as a way of life. As we read the Bible we find the law of God clearly set out, and David said, 'Oh, how I love Your law!' (Psalm 119:97). All humans should love God's law. But God's people, who are born of his Holy Spirit, are new creatures and have the law of God written upon their hearts.

We are told in the Scriptures that without holiness we cannot see God. Of course we know that the holiness we need is that which comes from the Lord Jesus Christ. No matter what we do, we cannot earn our salvation. But this does not mean that we can live as we like and expect to gain heaven. To be clothed in the righteousness of Christ means that we will live in obedience to the law of God day by day. The reason for obeying God's law is given: Jesus said, 'If you love Me, keep My commandments' (John 14:15). God's people keep the commandments because they love Jesus, the Lawgiver.

If God's people fall into continual sin, he may decide to bring that sin to an end, and so he chastens his people. He corrects his erring child as a parent corrects an erring son or daughter. And sometimes the correction hurts. But God will have us to be holy!

Many years ago I was trying to train our pet cat to keep off the roof of our car. Every morning I would find him sitting up there. Dirty paw marks would be over the car's bonnet — it was easy to follow his tracks up to the roof. I would give the cat a smack and he would jump down, but the next morning he would be up there again.

One morning, I decided to teach the cat a lesson he would never forget. The cat was happily sitting on the roof of the car, so I quietly got into the car and started the engine. The silly cat just sat there unconcerned with what was happening. I decided I would put the car into reverse and shoot backwards out of the garage. I knew the cat would be unable to stand up and would thump down over the front of the car. This, I thought, would frighten him so much that he would never climb up on the car roof again. I wouldn't have to wash away the marks of his paws any more.

This was my training scheme. However, without thinking, I put the car in forward gear, not reverse, and accelerated. The cat shot over the back of the car as the car roared forwards. Sadly there were two bicycles in front of the car. They just crumpled and several bricks in the front of the garage cracked. Also paint was scraped off the car, and the bumper bar was badly dented.

The next morning, the cat was once again up on the roof of the car and I decided to forget the matter. My cat-training scheme had failed miserably. I had been taught a lesson.

God chastens his people so that they might become better Christians. Of course some Christians fail to learn the lesson of the chastening. May that not be the case with you.

In Paul's first letter to the Corinthians (1 Corinthians 11:17-34) we read of some Christians who used the Lord's Supper as an opportunity for having a great party, where some people even became drunk. Because of this terrible sin, God took action to correct the people. We read, 'For he who eats and drinks in an unworthy manner eats and drinks judgement to himself, not discerning the Lord's body. For this reason many are weak and sick among you, and many are dead' (vv. 29-30).

It may be that the Lord is chastening you. If so, then rejoice, for it is a sign that God loves you and that he would have you depart from sin and be conformed more and more to the likeness of his Son, Jesus Christ.

Unlike my pathetic efforts to correct the wayward cat, God's chastening will always achieve its purpose. But always remember that God uses parents, schoolteachers, your minister and elders and many others — even grandparents — in the training of the young. You must always respect those who are placed in positions of trust. When they set you a fine example of Christian living, imitate them.

Always remember King David, who committed terrible sins. God punished him, as we have found out in our reading for today. Always remember that God never allows sin to go unpunished. He will have his people Christlike.

Activities

1. List five changes that should take place in the life of a person who becomes a Christian.
2. What story did Nathan tell David?
3. Why was David angry with the rich man?
4. What did Nathan's story teach David?

STORY 3

Don't leave the boat

Read

Acts 27:13-44

'For if we sin wilfully after we have received the knowledge of the truth, there no longer remains a sacrifice for sins, but a certain fearful expectation of judgement, and fiery indignation which will devour the adversaries. Anyone who has rejected Moses' law dies without mercy on the testimony of two or three witnesses. Of how much worse punishment, do you suppose, will he be thought worthy who has trampled the Son of God underfoot, counted the blood of the covenant by which he was sanctified a common thing, and insulted the Spirit of grace?' (Hebrews 10:26-29).

If you have read some of my other stories I'm sure you will realize that I like fishing. When I was young I spent many happy hours on the river-bank trying to catch the 'big one'. My brother is also a keen fisherman and often we would spend hours together catching a meal of fish.

During my teaching career, I was appointed to a small school situated on an island only a few miles from the mouth of a river that flowed into the Pacific Ocean. It wasn't long before I realized that here was my chance to catch the really big fish. So I bought a boat that I could use on the ocean. It wasn't a very big boat — about four metres long — but it had a powerful outboard motor and was very quick.

The big problem was how to get out to sea in such a small boat. My brother and I took the boat down to the beach on a day when the breaking waves weren't too high. We pushed the boat out into the water with the waves splashing about us, started the outboard engine and then waited for a lull in the waves. Then we jumped into the boat and headed for the wide blue ocean. It was a case of going full speed ahead. Sometimes if a large wave built up we would have to turn the boat for the shore and start all over again. Many people told us we were very foolish risking our lives to catch fish. However, we really did catch some very big fish.

One day my brother rang to ask if we could have a day's fishing. I was always happy to have John with me out on the sea. We packed a lunch for the day, made sure there was plenty of petrol in the tank and checked the fishing gear. My brother and I used to take a Bible and a psalm book with us. We were always worried that the engine might not start and we would need something to read while the coastguard looked for us — and what better than the Bible? But before we went out to sea we checked the weather forecast to make sure there would be no danger from strong winds springing up.

We slept well that night, arose well before sun-up, and had the boat on the beach just as the sky was beginning to glow from the rising sun. The waves looked somewhat bigger than at other times, but we thought all would be well. However, I remember my brother saying, 'Maybe we should call it off today. I think the waves are too big.'

'I don't think we have anything to worry about,' I replied.

We pulled the boat across the sand and launched it into the smaller waves at the water's edge. John held the boat steady while I jumped in and started the engine. When I thought there was a lull in the waves I shouted out, 'Jump in! We're going!' John clambered on board and we headed out for the ocean.

We made it through the first break in the waves, but about 300 metres from the shore we saw some huge ocean swells before us. Neither of us said a thing. We knew we had made a big mistake going out to sea on that particular day.

The first wave broke about twenty metres from the boat and by the time it hit us the boat took in about five centimetres of water. The next wave broke about fifteen metres from the boat and we found about thirty centimetres of water in the boat.

We just looked at one another in unbelief as the third wave broke on top of our boat. The engine then stopped and the boat was completely filled with water. The next wave was a huge one, and as the boat was beginning to lift on the swell, I dived overboard. The boat capsized and when the wave passed there we were — two very keen fishermen clinging to an upturned boat.

We couldn't believe what had happened, and we were worried. The shore was about 400 metres away and neither of us were good swimmers. I started to think about sharks and was afraid that our legs hanging down in the water would provide them with a great meal.

My brother said, 'I told you we shouldn't have tried to get out today. What are we going to do?'

We thought for a while and then John continued, 'We should stay with the boat. If we leave the boat and try to swim to shore we'll be drowned. Our wives will miss us when we don't come home and they'll get the coastguard out to look for us.'

We hung on to the boat in silence. Then John spoke again, this time with a laugh: 'Isn't there a hymn that has a line about the perils of the sea?'

After a little thought he began to sing, 'Rescue the perishing — care for the dying.' We then discussed Paul's shipwreck and decided that no matter what happened we would follow his God-given advice. We would stay with the boat — there was safety with the boat as it would not sink because of the buoyancy chambers. We were eventually caught in a current that swept us back to the beach. Two hours after capsizing, our feet touched the sand.

Now there is a great scriptural truth in this true story, and it is simply this. If we would be saved from our sins we must trust in the Lord Jesus Christ alone. We must cling to him, for there is no way to be rid of our sins except through his death on the cross — his death in our place.

It is very sad to know of people who once claimed to be Christians and now show no interest in the things of Christ. They attended church and Bible study groups and may even have taught in the Sunday Schools, but that is now all in the past. It is these people that the writer to the Hebrews says have 'trampled the Son of God underfoot, counted the blood of the covenant by which [they were] sanctified a common thing, and insulted the Spirit of grace'.

The truth is that there is no salvation outside of Jesus Christ. People may turn away from Christ and trust in whatever they like, but unless they trust in Jesus they are lost for ever. Some people think that if they live a 'good' life God will save them. But this is not so. There is only one sacrifice for sins and that is the sacrifice of Jesus on the cross at Calvary. And so we must stay with Christ in order to be saved — just as John and I knew we would be safe if only we stayed with the capsized boat.

One of the ways you can tell that your faith is God-given is when it lasts and lasts right to the very end of your life. Just as our feet touched the sand and we knew we were safe, so also a living faith will bring you finally to the heavenly shore. Life may be difficult, just as the waves proved a problem for our fishing effort, but God's care is ever about you.

So, my reader, put your trust in Jesus Christ as the only Saviour that God has provided. Stick to him through life's tempests and one day he will welcome you home — into the kingdom he has prepared for all of his people.

Activities

1. How does Jesus save a sinner from the punishment due to him because of sin?
2. What is meant by 'trusting Jesus'?
3. Name someone you trust and explain why you trust that person.
4. What is the true home of God's people?

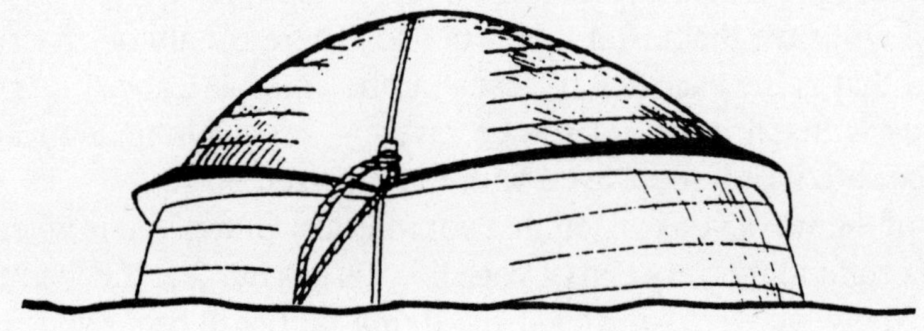

STORY 4

Snakes and graves

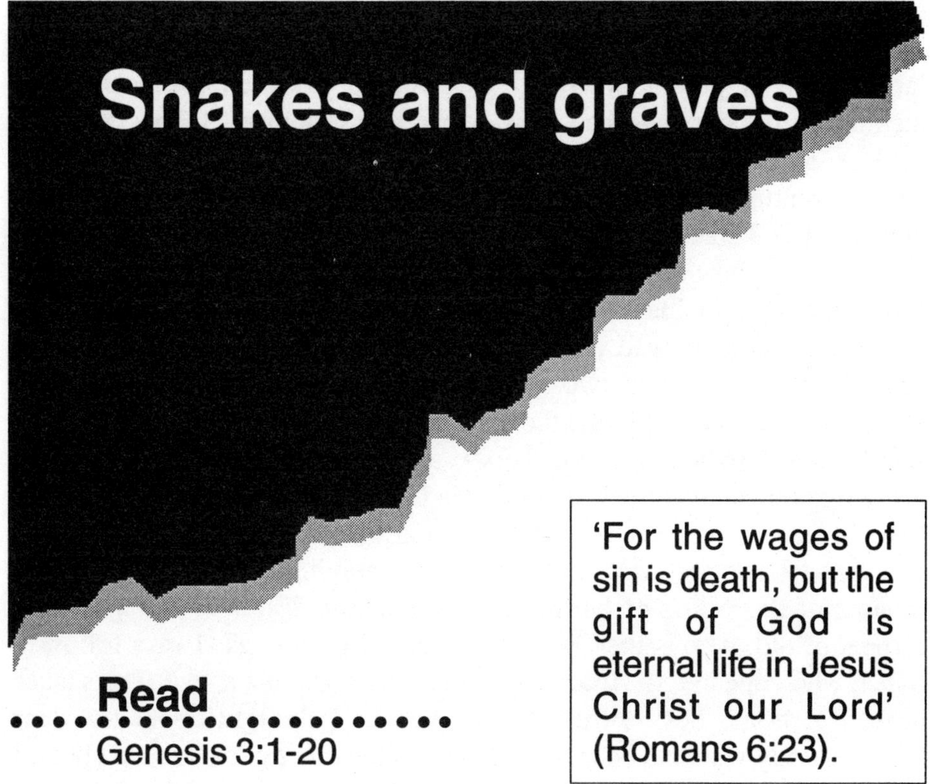

Read

Genesis 3:1-20

> 'For the wages of sin is death, but the gift of God is eternal life in Jesus Christ our Lord' (Romans 6:23).

Standing beside an open grave with a coffin containing the body of someone who has died is a reminder that, unless the Lord Jesus comes first, we also shall die. Christians should not fear death, because it is through death that we go to be with the Lord Jesus Christ, who loves us and gave himself for us. Dying can be very uncomfortable for some, but we must always remember that God has promised to give his people the grace needed to die well.

I conducted the funeral service of an old lady who was ninety-five years of age. She was a lovely Christian woman who suffered a lot during the last few years of her life. But she was always bright and uncomplaining. She had a strong faith in Christ as her Lord and Saviour. She faced death with confidence, knowing that she would go home to be with Jesus.

I was to conduct the burial service — beside the open grave. Now graveyards are not the nicest of places. They should remind us that the 'wages of sin is death' (Romans 6:23).

In your reading for today, you will have seen how Satan appeared to Eve in the form of a snake. He lied about God with the result that Eve and then Adam fell into sin. The very moment they disobeyed God, their bodies began to grow old and eventually they died. This has been the case with every person born, with the exception of Enoch and Elijah, who passed into heaven without dying.

Let us then go back to the funeral. I stood beside the grave and faced a large group of people who had gathered to pay their respects to the memory of the one who had died. I read the Scriptures, 1 Thessalonians 4:13-18, and while I was speaking about the resurrection I noticed several people pointing, and one even had a smile on his face. As I continued I wondered if I had said something funny without knowing it. Then I thought, 'Maybe they are pointing to some people they know.' I soon forgot about the incident and the service came to a conclusion.

Then someone moved very quickly up to me and made me turn round. There behind me, about two metres away, were three snakes. My wife Valerie later told me she saw them come out of a hole beside a grave. She said she was terrified they would crawl up to me as I spoke. However, they just wriggled about in the warm sun. Had I known they were there I'm sure I would have moved very quickly — I don't like snakes.

I stood back and watched the snakes playing near the graves and thought of the words of Scripture in Revelation 20:2: 'The dragon, that serpent of old, who is the Devil and Satan...' Death has always followed Satan, who appeared to Adam and Eve in the form of a snake. The snakes looked at home beside the graves. And as I thought about the dear Christian lady who had been buried, and all the other graves round about, I saw again the heartache that sin has caused.

'The wages of sin is death...' And there at that graveyard I could see the

evidence of the consequence of sin. To many people it would appear that death and the grave have the victory — that when a person dies, that is the end. But that is not so. For we are told that Christ will return and when he does he will bring with him the souls of those who have gone to be with him. These souls will be reunited with their resurrected bodies. In other words, the grave and death do not have the victory.

Jesus was crucified and died, but he rose again; and as surely as Jesus rose from the dead, so also all will rise again. For those who are not Christians their resurrection will be one of horror and shame. They will be judged and justly thrown into hell. But for God's people, we shall inherit the new heavens and the new earth, which will be our home for ever.

There are some wonderful words found in Revelation 21:3-4 which tell us something about God's home for his people. We read, 'And I heard a loud voice from heaven saying, "Behold the tabernacle of God is with men, and He will dwell with them, and they shall be His people, and God Himself will be with them and be their God. And God will wipe away every tear from their eyes; there shall be no more death, nor sorrow, nor crying; and there shall be no more pain, for the former things have passed away."'

Our God has the victory over the serpent and so also do all of Christ's people. Our text for today should give you great encouragement. All who live by faith in Jesus Christ have eternal life.

But how many people hear the gospel story and take no notice! Satan is ever at work distracting people from the good news concerning Christ. When I was speaking at the graveside, that was just what the snakes were doing — distracting the congregation from the preaching of the Word of God.

Do you have faith in Christ? Can you say with the apostle Paul, 'For to me, to live is Christ, and to die is gain...'? (Philippians 1:21). You can if you are a Christian!

Activities

1. What is meant by the words, 'The wages of sin is death'?
2. What will happen to our bodies when Jesus returns?
3. What do you think will be the most wonderful thing about heaven?

STORY 5

Three legs are better than four

Read

Matthew 5:27-30

'And if your right hand causes you to sin, cut it off and cast it from you; for it is more profitable for you that one of your members perish, than for your whole body to be cast into hell' (Matthew 5:30).

I'm sure that most of my readers have had a pet of one kind or another. I grew up on a farm and was always surrounded by plenty of animals. Of course my brother and I had special animals as pets. We even had a billy goat at one time. There were always pet cats to keep the mice and rats under control, but my favourite pet was usually a dog.

I had many dogs as pets. One particular dog I called Spot. He was a brown dog with a big black patch on his chest. When he was a pup I picked him out as my own. He and I were good mates. He would follow me everywhere I went. Soon he learned to run after a ball and bring it back. He was the best fielder when, with some of my friends, we played cricket. He would crouch down when the ball was bowled and then race after the ball when it was hit.

Sometimes he was a pest, as he would get the ball in his mouth and then look at everyone. He somehow knew that we wanted the ball to get on with the game. When we ran towards him to get the ball, he would run away. Sometimes it took minutes to catch him and get the ball back. There were times when we had to tie him up in order to have some peace. He would howl then as he really wanted to have his fun with the ball.

Spot had a very bad habit, however. He loved to chase bikes and cars. My brother and I used to ride our bikes to school, and Spot would trot along after us. We would have to shout out loudly at him, and sometimes we even threw stones at him to make him go back home. But he loved to chase cars and and try to bite their wheels. This was a very dangerous habit! Some drivers swerved to miss him but we were afraid he would be hit, or cause an accident.

We would give him a smack when he chased a car. He soon learned that when he chased a car he would be in trouble. But he just couldn't resist the temptation! He must have thought it was worth a smack for the fun of chasing cars along the road. I can remember Dad saying, 'If you boys don't train that dog we will have to get rid of him. Someone will end up being killed!' So my brother John and I did our best to stop him doing what was wrong. But it proved to be a waste of time.

Then one day Spot ran out after the milk truck. This time he misjudged the speed of the truck and it was Spot who was badly injured. He had a broken leg and the bones were poking through the flesh. He screamed out in pain, and John and I were very upset.

'What can we do for Spot?' I asked Dad.

'I think he'll have to be put down,' Dad replied.

But with a lot of pleading, Dad eventually agreed to take Spot to the vet. When the vet saw him he said that Spot's leg would have to be removed. Somehow Dad agreed and soon we had a three-legged dog. It took Spot a long time to recover, but he had learned his lesson. No longer did he chase cars!

But we had Spot and he was still alive and a good mate. He trotted after us when we went fishing, and he would help Dad round up the cows at milking time. So in some ways, as far as Spot was concerned, three legs were better than four. He now could not get himself into so much trouble.

Our text for today should remind us that sin is evil. God has commanded us to be holy, and this means turning away from our sinful habits and following Jesus. Jesus is telling his hearers that sometimes his people must take radical action to avoid sin. He likens that action to cutting off a hand or plucking out an eye. Jesus has commanded that we avoid swearing and telling wicked stories. Maybe you do not usually swear, but find that when you meet certain people you do. Jesus then is telling you to stop meeting those people. He is saying, 'Don't put yourself in those situations that cause you to sin.' Sometimes when you watch certain shows on the television it has a bad effect upon you. You then must turn off the TV.

I have a friend who loves to buy tools for his workshop, even though he knows he doesn't need them. He has told me that he 'covets' tools and that every time he passed a hardware shop he used to go in and have a look around. Many times, he would come out with some new tool. But he has overcome the sin of coveting in a simple way. He prayed to God asking that he might be forgiven his sin and now when he sees a hardware shop along the street, he crosses over to the other side. Now he does not even let himself be tempted. So also it must be with you.

Our text speaks about parts of our body that are good. We need our hands, feet and eyes, but like most things they can be used in a sinful way. I'm sure that many of my readers enjoy sport. There is no sin in playing sensible games, but what do you do when the coach tells you to act unfairly towards others? What are you going to do when the game you enjoy playing is going to be held on the Lord's Day?

There are times when you must make real sacrifices for your faithfulness to Christ. Serving and worshipping Jesus is the most important thing in the world, and we don't serve Jesus by sinning. So do all you can, with the help of God's Holy Spirit, to avoid sin and live a life of obedience to your Saviour, Jesus Christ.

Activities

1. Why was Spot better off with three legs than with four?
2. What did Jesus mean when he said, 'And if your right hand causes you to sin, cut it off and cast it from you; for it is more profitable for you that one of your members perish, than for your whole body to be cast into hell'?
3. God commands us to be 'holy'. What does this mean?

STORY 6

I like gifts!

Read

John 6:22-40

'All that the Father gives Me will come to Me, and the one who comes to Me I will by no means cast out' (John 6:37).

I'm sure that everyone enjoys receiving gifts. My own children and grandchildren love to receive presents, and when my children were young they would keep reminding us that it would soon be their birthday. As birthdays approached they would make sure we looked in the shop windows to have pointed out what they really would like as a gift. Even adults like to receive gifts and I'm sure that when birthdays draw near almost everyone looks forward to receiving presents.

Some time ago I made the mistake of telling my adult children that there was nothing I needed, or nothing I really wanted, for my birthday. I was so disappointed when they took seriously what I said. They rang up and wished me a happy birthday. They sent me funny birthday cards, but there were no gifts to open and enjoy. I complained to my wife, who passed on the message, and now I receive birthday gifts again.

So we all look forward to receiving gifts.

The Bible has something to say about gifts and our text for the day tells us that all who trust in Jesus Christ as their Saviour are the gift of the Father to his Son. This means that if we are Christians we are very special to Jesus and his Father. God has chosen a people to be saved from their sins. In eternity, before the world existed, God wrote the names of his people in the Lamb's book of life. The heavenly Father then gave those people to his Son. All Christians, who are called saints, are special people. And how Jesus loves those people who have been given to him!

Our text tells us that all who were given to Jesus would come to him. None of Christ's people ever wanted to go to him to be saved, but God made it possible for this to happen. He gave us the most wonderful gift of all — he gave his Son to be our Saviour. We read those lovely words in John 3:16: 'For God so loved the world that He gave His only begotten Son, that whoever believes in Him should not perish but have everlasting life.' Our God gave his Son to a hostile world, that he might save his people. He came into this world as a baby and in our place lived a life of complete obedience to God. Then he died upon a cross, bearing our sin. He received the punishment due to us for our sins. And because of his life and death he saved his people and sent the gift of the Holy Spirit.

Our text also tells us that all who are given by the Father to the Son will come to him. It is the Holy Spirit who shows us our sinfulness and our need of a Saviour. It is the Holy Spirit who gives us the gift of faith, making it possible to believe in Jesus as our Redeemer. It is the Holy Spirit who makes us hate our sins and seek forgiveness from God.

So all who trust in Jesus are the gift of the heavenly Father to the Son. If you are a Christian, you are very special to God. He chose you to be saved. You are very special to Jesus, because he loves you so much that he died to save you. And you are very special to the Holy Spirit, because he came and changed your heart, making it possible for you to trust in the Son of God. In John 17 we read the great prayer of Jesus before he left his disciples to be crucified. There we read Jesus' words to his Father that he would 'give eternal life to as many as You have given Him' (v. 2).

Don't ever say, 'I might not be one of those who have been given by the Father to the Son, so it doesn't matter what I do.' The Bible tells you to go to Jesus and ask for the Holy Spirit to be given to you so that you might believe.

Look at your text for today: the second part of it reads, 'And the one who comes to Me I will by no means cast out.'

Gifts are special. If you trust in Jesus you are very special to God. May God bless you!

Activities

1. What is the 'Lamb's book of life'?
2. What is a saint?
3. Learn the text of John 3:16.
4. Why did Jesus come into the world?

STORY 7

Simon loves the wrapping paper

Read Matthew 6:24-34

'Is not life more than food and the body more than clothing?' (Matthew 6:25).

I wonder just how much money people spend on their bodies? When we look about us we get the impression that the most important part of people is their body. When you walk into a home you find comfortable chairs in which the body can rest. In the bedroom there is a bed for the body to rest upon. Look in the wardrobe and there you will usually find fine clothing, not just to keep the body warm, but to make it look lovely. Have a look on the dressing table and there you will probably find some jewels, brooches, earrings, necklaces, tie-pins, cuff-links, and so on, to hang on the body.

If you look really hard I'm sure you will sometimes find lipstick, powder, rouge, eye-shadow, after-shave, hair-spray and many other things that are used in an effort to make the body look more beautiful. But that's not all. Bodies don't always smell the best, so you will also find perfume, sweet-smelling powder and underarm deodorant to give the body a nice smell.

Then out you go to the garage and there you find a car that is used to carry the body around. Most people work hard to be able to buy delicious food to keep the body alive. They use their hard-earned money to keep the body happy. For many people the most important part of their being is their body.

I have a grandson named Simon. When he was a baby we always made sure to buy him gifts that he would enjoy. But you will probably have experienced what happened to us.

I remember, one Christmas, buying Simon a toy police car that had flashing lights. When a button was pushed a siren would sound and a loud voice would say, 'Pull over!' Nan and I thought it would be just the most wonderful present.

When Christmas Day arrived the family met for the exchange of gifts and a meal together. Christmas was always a happy family time. When Simon's name was called out, he was given his police car, wrapped in colourful paper with a ribbon around it. He took it in his hands and looked hard. We watched and said, 'Come on, Simon, take the paper off and see what Nan and Pop have for you!' We wanted to see the expression of joy on his face as he saw the car and played with it. This didn't happen, however. Simon's hands crunched the wrapping paper, and a smile came to his face. The crunching sound of the paper seemed wonderful to him.

Well, we helped him unwrap the police car that we had so carefully chosen. I even pushed it along and made the siren sound. But Simon wasn't interested in the car. All he wanted to do was play with the colourful wrapping paper. Soon he was joined by two other grandchildren, Kim and Samantha. They saw the fun that Simon was having with his wrapping paper, so they also took their wrapping paper over to him and there they played for a long time. It was a bit of a let-down for Nan and Pop. After all, the things that mattered to us were the gifts inside the wrapping paper.

Now in our text and reading for today Jesus is warning his hearers that they are more than just bodies that need pampering. Our bodies are important. I know that my body is important to me, because I live in it. I keep my body clean, clothed, fed and in good health, because God gave me a body to live in. But the most important part of me is me — my soul! My soul will live for ever. It will never die.

If you want to be a friend of Jesus, and have Jesus as your Friend, your soul must be put right with God. Sin means that you are an enemy of God. You must turn to Christ and seek his forgiveness. You must trust in him for your salvation. More important than the feeding of your body is the feeding of your soul. Daily you must read God's Word and daily you must speak to God in prayer. If your soul is right with Jesus so also is your body. The Holy Spirit makes his home in your body and this is a wonderful truth.

Jesus reminds us in our Scripture passage to take care of our soul first of all — then we are to concern ourselves about the body. But always remember that our bodies wear out and will one day die, unless Christ returns first. Our bodies will return to the dust. But that is not the end. When Jesus comes again all of his people will be resurrected with glorious new bodies that will never wear out. Jesus saves us both body and soul.

So don't spend your life slaving to pamper your body, but work so that Christ might be glorified. Keep your body and mind healthy, but first of all make sure your soul is right with Jesus.

Don't be like Simon, who thought that the best part of the present was the wrapping. While you are still at school, do the very best in your studies so that you might serve Jesus better in your daily life. Learn to read, so that you might be able to read the Bible and so feed your soul. When you are older and work, either at home or in the workplace, always do your best. In this way Christ is glorified. And if you earn money from your work, then remember to give to the Lord, so that the gospel message might be spread and other people saved.

Activities

1. What will happen to your body when you die?
2. What happens to a Christian's soul when he or she dies?
3. How can you nourish your soul?

STORY 8

I enjoy water melons

Read

Matthew 7:15-20

'By their fruits you will know them' (Matthew 7:20).

As I have already mentioned, my brother John and I grew up on a farm. Farm life was hard at times. The cows had to be milked twice a day, so someone had to be home every day to do the work. It was almost impossible to have a real holiday. But we had a lot of fun growing up on a farm. There were horses to ride, birds to trap, rabbits to catch, a river for fishing, boats to row about in, animals to play with and a freedom that most city people never really know.

But, even when we were young, there were jobs we had to do. As I grew older, the hard life on the farm didn't appeal any more. I wanted to become a schoolteacher, which I did, and so did my brother. My wife was also a farmer's daughter. She too found farm life hard and became a schoolteacher.

However, after Valerie and I were married we always liked growing our own vegetables. It reminded us of the good old days when there was plenty of fresh fruit and vegetables to be eaten. We dug up our garden and planted tomatoes, beans, peas, lettuce and lots of other vegetables.

Every spring my wife used to plant half a dozen water-melon seeds, and by the time the summer weather arrived we usually had beautiful red water melons to eat. Even now it makes my mouth water, thinking of the cool water-melon juice running down my throat — and down my face and neck.

As well as the water melons, Valerie carefully saved the seeds from other plants, including a delicious pumpkin and a rock melon. Last year she decided to plant a few seeds once again. I have given up growing vegetables, as I think it costs more to grow your own than to buy frozen vegetables from the shop. But Valerie's seeds always produced great vegetables.

'They were lovely melons last year,' she said. 'With these seeds the melons this year will be just as good. I've given some to our church friends. They might as well enjoy them.'

A couple of weeks after planting, the small plants had broken through the ground. They were very healthy plants and soon strong trailing stems, or vines, were beginning to cover the ground. Several times a week we watered the growing plants and gave them the very best manure to help them on their way. Some weeks later flowers began to appear and we could see the bees busy pollinating the flowers. Everything was looking just right. When we asked our friends how their crop was coming on, one said, 'I've just planted the water melons. The vines are really growing. We're looking forward to a feast in the summertime.'

We decided to visit them and see how their plants were going. But when Valerie saw them she said, 'They're not water melon vines. They're pumpkin vines.'

'But,' replied Jack, 'Leanne carefully marked all the seeds and I'm sure I planted the water-melon ones.'

But Valerie just smiled again and said, 'I don't think you'll have water melons. These are pumpkin vines. I think you must have mixed up your seeds.'

Jack looked at the growing plants and said, 'I'm sure they were the water-melon seeds I planted.'

'Well,' replied Valerie, 'when the fruit appears you will then know the truth.'

Each Sunday we would have a report on the plants. Soon there were flowers and then small fruit appeared. But my wife, who knows more about plants, kept telling me, 'I'm sure they are not water melons they have growing.' I just wasn't sure, so could offer no sensible advice.

Then, one day, we called in to have a look at the so-called water melons. But Valerie was right — they had a lovely crop of pumpkins. That year we shared our water melons with Jack and Leanne and they gave us some of their pumpkins. We took special care that in future we put the seeds in envelopes and wrote the names of each in big letters. We didn't make that mistake again. The water-melon and pumpkin plants look very similar to the city gardener, but you can't make the mistake when you see the fruit on the vine.

Jesus, in our text and reading for today, reminds us that good trees produce good fruit and that poor trees produce bad fruit. We can tell what type of tree it is by looking at and tasting the fruit. So it is with the prophets, who spoke to the people about God. Some prophets were true prophets who spoke the Word of God with sincerity — and always spoke the truth, warning the people that they needed to repent of their sins and trust in Christ for their salvation. Then there were false prophets, who told lies about the way of salvation and led people astray. How were the ordinary people to tell who was a true prophet and who was a false prophet? Jesus told them to observe what type of people the prophets were. Did they live a life of obedience to God's laws? Did they show true love for one another? Did they love God? The same applies today. There are many people who pretend to be ministers of Christ. They preach sermons using wonderful words. Should you follow them? Should you believe what they say?

Well, check them out! Compare what they are saying with the teachings found in the Bible. If they do not teach what the Bible teaches, don't follow them! If they are not living a holy life, then don't follow them, for God's people will live in such a way and speak such words that Christ is glorified. By their fruit you will know them!

And what about you? Do you tell people that you are a follower of Christ and then by your words and life show that you are no different from anyone else in the world? By your fruit, you will be known.

Our Scripture passage reminds us that if we are not true to our profession of faith in Christ, we shall be cut down like a useless tree and thrown into the fires of hell. Reader, may your faith be a living faith, and may you always do the works of faith.

Activities

1. How could the Jewish people work out who were true prophets of God?
2. Today, how can you determine if a person is speaking God's truth?
3. What are some of the fruits that should be found in the life of a Christian?

STORY 9

Lost and found

Read

Luke 15:1-10

> 'Rejoice with me, for I have found the piece which I lost' (Luke 15:9).

Some years ago my wife and I, with our two youngest daughters Lisa and Cathie, had a holiday in Hong Kong. We had never been overseas before and decided we would like to see a people and culture that would be completely different from those in Australia.

We had a wonderful time looking over the city. We learned how to bargain for goods and saw sights we had never seen before. We had a ride on a sampan (a small boat), travelled in a cable car to the top of a mountain peak, took bus trips here and there, and generally had a great time.

We all wanted to make a trip into mainland China. We could only afford a one-day trip, so we booked our fares. It meant travelling to Macau on a ferry, being met by a bus and then taken across the border into Communist China.

It was a fine day when we set out early to catch the ferry to Macau. The ferry was a hydrofoil and moved very quickly across the sea to its destination. There were quite a few tourists with us on the ship, as well as a guide who spoke both English and Chinese. Everyone was very excited about the day that was coming up. Cathie and Lisa were talking to some other young folk about what they hoped to see and do.

After about half an hour the ferry docked at the very large wharf in Macau. The guide told everyone to wait till the crowd thinned out and then we would get through the immigration section with ease. However, I was very keen to get off the boat, get through the immigration gates and then take a photograph of my wife and two children as they passed through the entrances.

I told my wife what I intended to do, and she said, 'Be careful. You're in a foreign country.' Then she said, 'I think you should stay with us. You can get photographs later on.' But I was determined that I would get those special photographs.

After telling the family I would meet them outside the immigration gates, I moved off the boat with the great numbers of people who were visiting Macau. I just followed the crowd. Quickly I had my passport checked and was waiting with camera at the ready to photograph the family coming through the customs and immigration section.

But a few minutes later the crowd had thinned out and still the family had not arrived. I waited quietly for another few minutes and there seemed to be very few people about. I could also see the ferry we had travelled on moving out from the wharf. I began to get worried.

'Where is everyone?' I thought to myself. 'I couldn't have missed them.' Then I found a man in a uniform and asked where tourists usually went after going through the immigration gates. He just waved his arms about and spoke something in Chinese. I was getting a sinking feeling in my stomach. I didn't know what to do.

Then I thought I had better leave the wharf area and move to any place where there were buses. When I left the enclosed area there were no buses to be seen. I knew that I was lost and everyone spoke Chinese. I began to pray that I might find my way out of the mess I was in. Looking about desperately, I tried to see Valerie or the girls — or anyone who looked like an English-speaking tourist. After I had been standing in the same area for about twenty minutes a Chinese man came up to me. He was dressed in a smart uniform. He looked me in the eyes and asked, 'Are you Jim?'

I was overjoyed. When I told him I was, he said, 'Come with me. The bus is waiting for you!'

When we reached the waiting bus a great cheer went up from the passengers and I hung my head in shame. My two daughters looked at me in a way that I knew meant they weren't very pleased with their father.

'How did I miss you?' I asked Valerie.

'You should have stayed with us,' Valerie replied. The guide took us through a special set of gates for tourists. When we were all on the bus the driver asked, 'Is everyone here?' Then Lisa told him that her father was missing. We were so embarrassed. 'Don't go off by yourself again. Stay with us and you won't get lost.' I felt like a naughty little boy!

Every time we boarded the bus after stopping for a look at various places in China, the driver used to look at my wife and daughters and ask, 'Is your father here, or do I have to go and find him again?'

That night, when I was safely back in the hotel room in Hong Kong, I laughed about the incident. But when we arrived home from our holiday, everyone was told about the day I was lost.

And that is what our Bible reading for today is about: a lost sheep and a lost coin. The owner of the sheep thought a lot about that one lost sheep. He looked and looked till he found it. Then he returned it to the flock. The same was the case with the lost coin. That one coin was very important to the woman. She searched the house till she found it.

Jesus was telling his listeners that men and women are lost in sin. And so lost are we that we can do nothing to find ourselves. We don't even know that we are lost. We don't even want to be found, until the Holy Spirit changes our hearts.

When I was lost in Macau, I could do nothing to help myself. But someone who loved me made sure that I was found.

Reader, if you are one of Christ's people, if you are loved by him, if he died to save you, he will find you. The Holy Spirit will change your heart and give to you the gift of faith. You will repent of your sins and begin to live a life of godliness. If you already trust in Jesus, thank him for searching you out and saving you. If you are not a Christian, why not ask Jesus to send his Spirit into your heart so that you might trust yourself to him?

Activities

1. Where is Hong Kong?
2. What are we taught in the parable of the lost coin?
3. Who are the 'lost sheep' in the parable of the lost sheep?

STORY 10

A step between life and death

Read

1 Samuel 20:1-3,24-34

'There is but a step between me and death' (1 Samuel 20:3).

Now that I have been forced to retire from the ministry because of a back injury, my wife and I live in a small country town. It is a very pleasant town in which to live. Our street is very quiet and my wife and I love gardening. Because of my back problem she mows the lawn and digs up the garden. My job is to water the plants and cut the flowers.

Our neighbours are also good gardeners and there is always plenty of colour in the gardens. Because of the flowers and trees there are many birds in the area.

One neighbour goes to a lot of trouble to encourage the birds to visit his garden. He has bird baths on his lawn and he regularly feeds them. When he opens his back door quite a lot of birds fly towards his garden, thinking it is feeding-time.

My wife and I enjoy sitting on our side verandah watching the many birds flying from tree to tree. The birds that amaze us most of all are the parrots. They have the most beautiful colours. Their feathers are bright reds, blues, yellows and greens — and a host of other colours in between. We throw seed and scraps out into the garden and some birds are becoming very tame. Maybe one day they will come and feed out of our hands.

I remember being on a picnic with Valerie not long after we were married. We were in one of the National Parks having a barbecue. Our plates were covered with food when a kookaburra flew down out of a tree and grabbed the meat from my plate. He was very tame and I'm sure he had stolen food from many other people. His action gave me a terrible fright.

I thought no one would believe our story, so my wife put a sausage on her fork and held it out to the bird that was sitting on a branch above, waiting and watching. I then took the camera, and soon had a photograph of the bird taking the sausage from the fork. Maybe the birds in our garden will become like the one in the National Park. I hope so.

However, back to my story! We watch the birds eating and flying about in our yard. Sometimes there are fights over food and the best place to perch is on the branch of a tree. But the world of the birds always seems to be a happy and contented one.

One evening, when the sun was setting I heard the sound of something smashing into one of the large glass windows on the verandah. My wife and I jumped to our feet to find out what had happened. There on the verandah table lay a parrot. It wasn't moving. I picked the brightly coloured bird up and its head fell to one side. Its neck was broken and it was well and truly dead. One moment it was a living, flying, happy bird and within a second it was dead.

These sort of incidents don't just happen in the world of birds and animals, but again and again we hear of healthy people dying in an instant. Accidents are very common. None of us can be sure what the next moment holds for us. David's words in our text are very true: 'There is but a step between me and death.'

In our reading for today we learn of Saul's hatred of David. Saul wanted David dead and went out of his way to try to capture the future King of Israel. We also read of the wonderful friendship that existed between David and Saul's son Jonathan.

Remember that you must be prepared to meet God at any moment, for today may be the day when you are called into his presence. There is only a heartbeat between being alive on earth and standing before the Lord Jesus Christ, who is the King of kings and the Lord of lords.

Reader, are you ready for that meeting?

Activities

1. Who was David?
2. Why did Saul hate David?
3. How can you prepare for death and your meeting with God?

STORY 11

Taking the plunge

> 'Today, if you will hear His voice, do not harden your hearts...' (Hebrews 3:7-8).

Read

Matthew 19:16-26

When I was a schoolteacher, there were many times I took children camping. The schools in the district were using a church camp beside the ocean as a spot for weekly camps. Each year we took groups of boys and girls aged from eight to twelve years for a five-day holiday by the ocean. They learned to live together, play together and work together. We had many nature rambles along the beach and through the trees that lined the seaside. The children also studied the marine life in rock pools. Then there was a night for camping out.

I usually went with a group of about twenty boys. We had a four-wheel-drive car towing a trailer filled with our camping gear. There were tents, sleeping bags, cooking gear, eating utensils and all the other things that make camping exciting. On our first few camps we cooked over an open fire. But burnt sausages and blackened toast didn't go down so well. I then brought along my own gas barbecue. Our meals improved greatly after that.

After our evening meal we sang camp-fire songs in the light of the roaring fire. Of course there was always a hair-raising story before bedtime. Then as the coldness set in we would make our way to the tents. The boys were always very excited and it usually took a long time for everyone to settle down and get some sleep.

Of course some were awake early in the morning and did their best to wake everyone else up. The fire would be stoked and the boys would sit around the warm flames talking about the exciting night out in the bush. After packing all the supplies we set out back to the huts where everyone had a shower and changed clothes ready for the day's activities.

One day we decided to take a different route through the bush, back to the camp. It was a new bush track and the four-wheel-drive car with the trailer led the way. Before long the car came to a very old wooden bridge across a river. The driver stopped the car and got out to have a look at the safety of the bridge.

The boys who had been walking and jogging along after the car were there to give their advice. Everyone had a look at the wooden planks that crossed the river. Some thought it might be safe to cross, but others said that the timber was rotten and would break under the weight of the car and trailer.

We all stood there and talked for a while. The driver said he would try to turn the car round and go another way, but another teacher said, 'I'm sure it will be safe. The timber is not that bad. Let's try!'

Most of the boys said, 'Yes, Sir, give it a go!'

So we trusted ourselves to that wooden bridge. I think that some of the boys were hoping that the planks would give way, but slowly the car edged its way over the bridge and finally reached the safety of the opposite bank of the river. Everyone cheered!

Now, reader, there comes a time in the life of every person who hears the gospel story when a decision must be made. You either turn away and go your own way through life, or you commit yourself to the Lord Jesus Christ and trust your eternal salvation to him. You should step out in faith and say to Christ, 'Lord Jesus, I cannot save myself, but I am willing to give myself to you, for you are strong and I know you can save me from my sins.'

But you must make that first step of faith, for no one else can do that for you. I remember reading somewhere some very sad, but true words: 'The pathway to hell is paved with good intentions.' How many people today are in hell — people who thought that they would follow Christ some other time, and never had another time!

Our reading for today is of a young man who was concerned about his soul. He wanted eternal life. So concerned was he about his relationship with God that he went to Jesus for help. His intentions were excellent, but...! He had a real problem. He was very wealthy and loved his wealth more than he loved his own soul and eternal life.

I don't know what happened to that young man. I only hope that some time later he came to his senses, repented of his sin and followed Jesus Christ as Lord and Saviour of his life. He had to 'take the plunge' and turn from his worldly possessions and commit himself to Jesus.

Reader, have you done so? Jesus bids you come today and trust in him. He asks you to show your love for him by obedience to his commands. Where do you stand? Is the pathway you are walking paved with good intentions alone? I pray that it is not so!

Activities

1. What is the most exciting part of camping out?
2. How can you show God that you love Jesus?
3. What is meant by 'faith in Jesus Christ'?

STORY 12

A hole in the tank

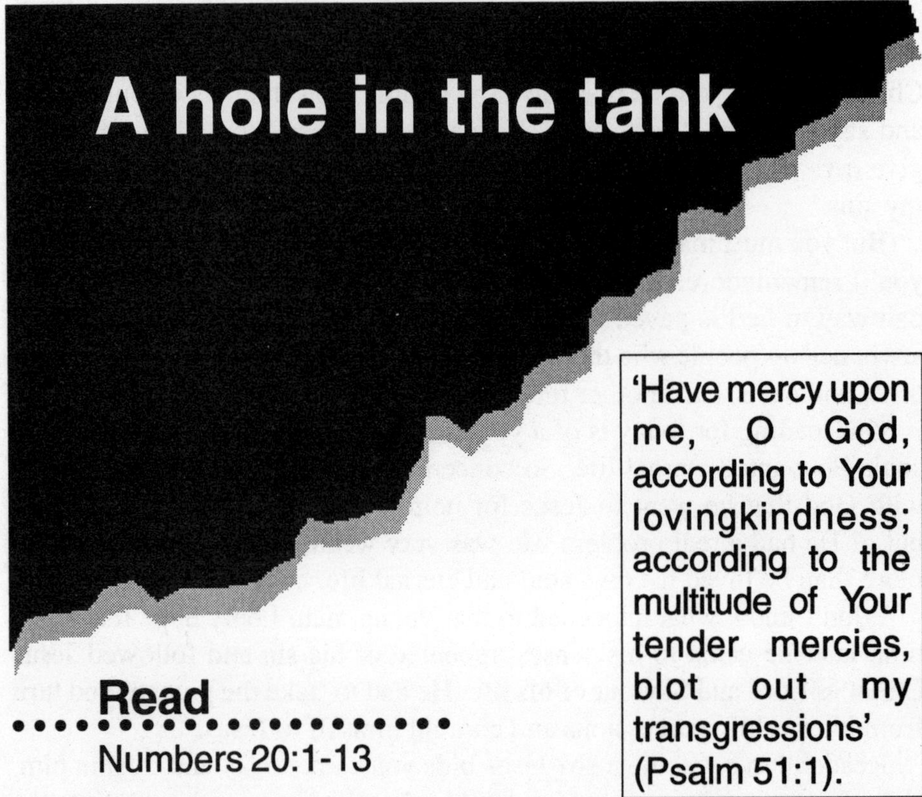

Read

Numbers 20:1-13

'Have mercy upon me, O God, according to Your lovingkindness; according to the multitude of Your tender mercies, blot out my transgressions' (Psalm 51:1).

Everything we do has consequences. Pass an exam and you are praised; break a window and you get into trouble. Eat green peaches and you will probably have pains in the stomach; have a good sleep and you will usually wake up refreshed.

There are times when we plan to act in a certain way, knowing that the consequences will be great. Sometimes we do things that have bad results. The Bible tells us of the consequences of sin. Sin brings physical death, and sin that is not repented of brings eternal death. This is a terrible consequence. But the Bible tells us that if we trust in the Lord Jesus Christ and confess our sins we shall be saved.

When I was a teacher in a small country school there were always plenty of snakes around in summer. One afternoon after school finished for the day, I saw a snake on a water tank beside our home. I called Valerie. As soon as she came outside to look, the snake crawled up the downpipe and into the guttering around the roof. The snake was a red-belly black snake and they are poisonous. I didn't like the idea of a snake being up in the house guttering. When we saw it duck under the tin roof and disappear from sight I said to my wife, 'I'm not going to sleep in the house until I see that snake come out!'

But Valerie replied, 'The snake can't get into the rooms. It can stay up in the roof for ever and it won't bother us.'

But I wasn't so sure and decided to do something about it. I took my rifle and climbed up on the roof of the house and waited for the snake to come out. Valerie said, 'Snakes like music, so I'll get the radio and bring it outside. That will bring the snake out.'

Out came the radio and there I was sitting on the ridge-capping of the roof waiting for a snake to come out to the music. I wasn't very confident about anything happening. But I was certain I would not sleep in the house till I was sure the snake was gone.

After about fifteen minutes of music I noticed a black head appear from under the roof. I put the rifle to my shoulder and waited. Slowly the snake came out into the guttering. It looked about in all directions. I took very careful aim at its head and pulled the trigger. I was surprised at my accuracy! The bullet hit the snake and it fell to the ground. Valerie came out and said, 'Well done! You'll be able to sleep in a bed tonight.' I climbed down from the roof and came over to the very still snake. I was very pleased with my shooting.

But everything a person does has consequences. Valerie was standing beside the snake. Then she pointed to the water tank and said, 'Look what you have done!' I looked towards the tank. But I really didn't have to look to know what had happened. Water was pouring out of the side of the tank. Up on the roof I was only concerned about the snake. I hadn't taken notice of what was behind it.

Well, we lost about half a tank of water before we could plug the hole. That water tank was our only supply for the house. I should have taken more care with what I was doing.

Our Bible reading for today is the story of Moses, that great man of God who led the Israelites out of the land of Egypt. He was longing to take God's people to the promised land, but he sinned. When there was no water for the Israelites to drink God told Moses to go and speak to a rock

and water would flow from it. But Moses was angry with the people because of their continual complaining. In anger he went to the rock and struck it twice with his rod. Water flowed and both the people and their animals had plenty to drink.

But Moses had sinned against God. God told him to speak to the rock, but Moses struck the rock. This action had a terrible consequence as far as Moses was concerned. God would now not allow him to lead the Israelites into the promised land.

The consequence of sin is death, but the apostle John wrote some wonderful words: 'If we confess our sins, He is faithful and just to forgive us our sins and to cleanse us from all unrighteousness' (1 John 1:9). Isn't this a wonderful promise? If we who love the Lord Jesus Christ confess our sins the consequence is that God will forgive us.

Reader, take notice of the warnings and promises of Scripture. All the warnings and promises have consequences. May God bless you!

Activities

1. Can you think of something you have done that had a wonderful consequence? Discuss it.
2. Why did Moses strike the rock?
3. The action of Moses was sinful. Why?
4. The Israelites entered Caanan, the promised land. What is the promised land for all of God's people?

STORY 13

Pruning produces great fruit and flowers

Read

John 15:1-8

'By this My Father is glorified, that you bear much fruit' (John 15:8).

My wife Valerie enjoys gardening. Each season new plants go into the well-prepared soil and before long we have flowers everywhere. In days gone by we also had a vegetable garden, but since our family has left home we don't bother with the vegetables. But we do have a lemon tree, an orange tree and a grapefruit tree. We also have two vines that produce fruit. There is a passionfruit vine which has lovely fruit, but even better than that is the grape vine.

My job in the garden, following my back injury, is to water the plants and give directions how Valerie should best do the work. I like to treat the plants with loving-kindness. However, we have had several trees that didn't do so well. They only produced a few flowers and the apple tree produced several apples that were eaten by worms. I told the trees that if they didn't do better the following year they would be cut out. The next year they disappeared from our garden.

One day after I had been away from home I returned to find that almost half the beautiful red-flowered bougainvillaea was missing. I parked the car in the garage and as I walked through the back garden I noticed that our two-metre-high grapevine was only about sixty centimetres high. I walked

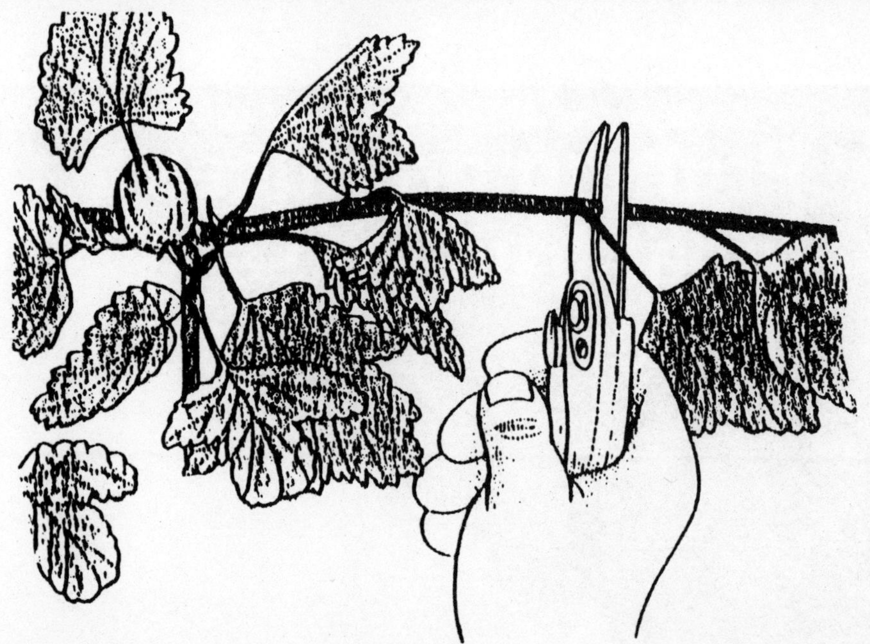

inside and asked Valerie, 'Whatever made you prune those vines so harshly? You've cut them back so much I think they'll die. We'll never get any grapes off that vine.'

But Valerie replied, 'I had a good look at both vines and there was so much dead wood on them I had to cut them back to the living wood. You wait and see. There'll be plenty of flowers on the bougainvillaea and the grapevine will be covered with bunches.'

I was a bit doubtful, but Valerie was the gardener. She knew the names of all the plants and had read a lot of books about gardening. I was just the person who held the hose and gave advice. We gathered all the dead wood and took it to the rubbish tip. It was good for nothing. It was winter time when our married daughters and their families visited us. I pointed out to them the well-pruned vines that I was sure would never produce anything.

Then came the first day of spring. The spring flowers were in full bloom and the bees were everywhere. Valerie called me to the front garden and pointed to the bougainvillaea.

'Have a look at that,' she said. There was new growth all over the bougainvillaea. I hadn't noticed the growth before. It looked as if there would be more flowers on the vine than ever before. My predictions of gloom were not going to be fulfilled.

Then Valerie said, 'Now I'd like you to have a close look at the grapevine.' Before we reached the grapevine I had a sinking feeling that I was going to be proved wrong again. Sure enough there was growth everywhere and five tiny bunches of grapes were forming. There was no doubt that cutting off the dead wood was the best thing that could have happened to those plants. This summer looks like producing our best crop of grapes and the bougainvillaea will look better than ever. I know that my daughters and their families will remind me of my words of doom for the plants. At least I know how to water plants. But I don't think I'll offer much gardening advice in the future!

Our reading for today is a reminder that as Christians we will produce much fruit. All who are united to the Lord Jesus Christ by faith are like the branches of a vine. As the branch receives its life-giving food from the stem, so also a Christian lives the Christian life because he or she is united by faith to Christ the Lifegiver. The fruit that Christians produce is the fruit of the Spirit. Paul wrote to the Galatians and said, 'But the fruit of the Spirit is love, joy, peace, longsuffering, kindness, goodness, faithfulness, gentleness, self-control...' (Galatians 5:22-23). In other words, there will be such evidences as a prayerful life, a desire to read the Bible and the heartfelt longing to be obedient to the commands of God.

The church members here on earth are like the branches on our grapevine. Some branches were dead and useless. They had never produced fruit. Others needed a little pruning to help them produce better fruit. Some branches were pruned hard so that they would produce even better fruit. The branches that were dead were just hanging onto the vine, but not attached to the stem. They were removed and cast into the rubbish and burned. There are people in the church who think they are Christians, but their life shows no fruit. Others produce a little fruit and some produce a lot of fruit. Now which are you? Can people tell by the way you live that you are attached to the one you say is your Saviour and Lord? Our reading for today reminds us that unfruitful professing Christians will be like the branches of the vine that were dead. They will be cast into the fires of hell.

Reader, where do you stand today? Is your life a testimony to the grace of God in your life? Or are you a big hypocrite, trying to fool others into believing that you belong to Jesus. Take seriously the words of Christ in Matthew 7:21: 'Not everyone who says to Me, "Lord, Lord," shall enter the kingdom of heaven, but he who does the will of My Father in heaven.' May God have so changed your life that you produce much spiritual fruit and so have that assurance in your life that you belong to Jesus. Faith is seen in a life of faithfulness.

Activities

1. Why are trees and vines pruned?
2. List the fruit of the Spirit. Now learn Galatians 5:22-23.
3. Think of a Christian you admire. Talk about some of the fruit you can see in that person's life.

STORY 14

Getting rid of stains

Read

Psalm 51:1-7

'But if we walk in the light as He is in the light, we have fellowship with one another, and the blood of Jesus Christ His Son cleanses us from all sin' (1 John 1:7).

When my wife and I had a holiday in Thailand some time ago, we were taken on a tour of a silk factory. First we were taken to a section where we could see silkworms hard at work. They were eating mulberry leaves and getting fatter every day. Some were spinning cocoons of golden silk thread. We were then taken to a spot where some women were unravelling the thread from the cocoons. It seemed to be a slow, hard job, but the ladies knew what they were doing and a lot of silk thread soon appeared. We then watched the weaving of the thread into silk material. The work was delicately done by hand and finally we saw the finished silk cloth.

Later we found ourselves watching workers making silk umbrellas. They were making the umbrellas out of cane and then covering the cane with the silk. Half a dozen artists then painted beautiful scenes on the umbrellas. Large fans were also made and these had glorious flowers and scenes painted on them. My wife and I bought a small umbrella and fan as souvenirs.

When we returned to Australia we found our mulberry tree covered with leaves, but there were no silkworms. However, on the tree there were thousands of mulberries. Most were a shiny black and ready for eating. We both stood under the tree and picked away, eating as many as we could. But we also picked a lot of the sweet berries to be made into pies. Mulberry pie with cream and ice cream is really great for supper!

If you have ever picked mulberries you will know that your hands will have a black stain on them. Soap won't get rid of the stain and it just has to wear off. The stain from the ripe, black berries was a nuisance. We were always searching for something to get rid of it.

One day Valerie came to me when I was working in the study and said, 'I want to show you something. You know how we are always having problems with the mulberry stain. I now know how to get rid of the stain.'

I stood up and followed her out to the mulberry tree.

'Here,' she said. 'Squash this berry in your fingers and I'll show you how to get rid of the stain.'

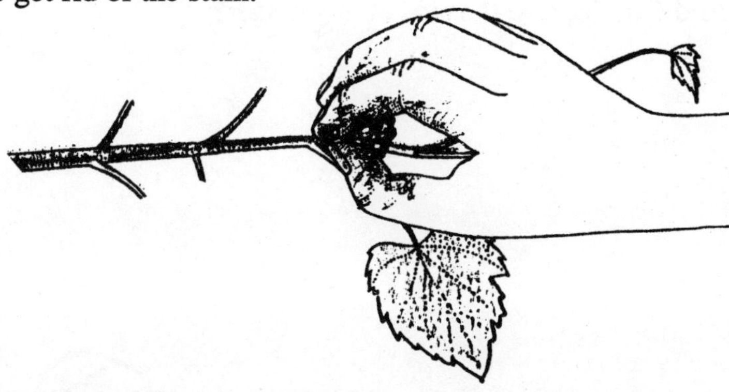

I did as I was asked, wondering if some terrible joke was about to be played on me. There was soon plenty of black mulberry stain on my fingers. Then Valerie gave me a green mulberry and said, 'Now squash this berry and rub the juice on the stain on your fingers.'

The deep black mulberry stain just disappeared from my fingers and hand. It was so easy I could hardly believe it.

Our reading for today speaks about sin. Sin is like that mulberry stain. It stains our bodies and souls. No matter what you do, you will never be able to remove the stain of sin. You might try to live a good life and go to church every Sunday, but that will not remove the stain of sin from your soul and body.

But, praise God, the Bible has the answer to the stain of sin! Reader, our text for today tells us a great and wonderful truth. We read again, 'The blood of Jesus Christ ... cleanses us from all sin.' Here is the answer to the stain of sin upon our souls and bodies. Jesus died so that our sins might be blotted out. He lived and died in the place of his people so that each one might be forgiven and clothed in his perfect righteousness. The prophet Isaiah wrote, '"Come now, and let us reason together," says the LORD, "though your sins are like scarlet, they shall be as white as snow; though they are red like crimson, they shall be as wool"' (Isaiah 1:18). Jesus Christ is the answer to the stain of sin. Only he can remove your sins and this he does when you, by his grace, trust in him.

Are you still covered with the stain of your own sins, or have you repented of your sins and cast yourself upon Christ for mercy? If you have truly repented and now live by faith in the Son of God for your salvation, you know that you have been cleansed from all unrighteousness.

Activities

1. Find Thailand in your atlas.
2. What are some of the ways that people try to remove the stain of sin?
3. Why should God forgive the sins of any sinner?

STORY 15

New glasses

Read

Matthew 16:1-20

> 'But the natural man does not receive the things of the Spirit of God, for they are foolishness to him; nor can he know them, because they are spiritually discerned' (1 Corinthians 2:14).

Many years ago, when I was in my late twenties, my wife noticed that I was holding a book at arm's length in order to read the words. At that time I was teaching in a small country school and doing university studies. I had to spend a great deal of time at my books and it was becoming noticeable to others that my arm was not long enough for easy reading.

I didn't like the idea of getting spectacles, but at long last was forced to do so. The optician gave me a prescription and later I walked out of a shop with my new glasses. I bought what I thought was a very flash pair of glasses. They had a lovely black frame — schoolteacher black. Not many other people thought my choice of frames was very good, but at least I could read much more easily.

My daughter Heather studied at university and became an optician. One of the first things that happened when she began work was to suggest that I get rid of my lovely black-rimmed glasses and get a new pair. To keep the family happy I agreed and once again everyone thought I looked respectable.

I used the glasses only for reading, but Heather then declared in her most professional voice that I needed glasses for long-distance sight as well. This time I had to have a nice gold-framed pair which were bifocals. I remember Heather telling me I would have to get used to this new type of lens — that I would have to persevere with them for a while and soon everything would look great again. And persevere I did, until two days later I walked to the front steps of the manse, became confused with the distance the steps were away, and fell down six steps without touching a step. It had been raining and I was dressed in good clothes as I was going out to visit a member of my congregation. Valerie ran to my aid, helped me to my feet and took me inside the house so I could clean up.

I decided that those glasses were no good for me. But when I told my daughter about my fall, she suggested getting multifocal lenses. This really solved my problems. I could see everything in focus at last. I didn't have to change my glasses when I stopped reading and wanted to see something in the distance. The world looked new! Everything was in focus!

I was reminded of the time when I wasn't hearing things so well and decided to visit the doctor. I thought I was going deaf. And Valerie was concerned as I never seemed to hear her call out, 'It's time for washing up!' The doctor washed the wax out of my ears, and I can still remember walking out of the surgery and hearing things I hadn't heard for ages. I could hear stones cracking under my shoes. I could even clearly hear birds singing. After we had finished tea that night, I heard Valerie call me to help with the washing up.

I'm sure my readers know that there are times in our lives when we can't make good sense of the world about us, because our eyesight is failing or our hearing is not as good as it used to be. With the proper help our problems are solved. In our text for today Paul tells his readers that ordinary people do not understand the truth of the Bible, which is the Word of God, because they are spiritually blind. Indeed, the ordinary person does not truly understand the truth of a sermon, because he or she is spiritually deaf. In order to properly understand the truth of God's Word you must be born again. It is God's Spirit who gives you an understanding of the Scriptures. Spiritual truths are 'spiritually discerned' (1 Corinthians 2:14).

In today's reading Christ called the Pharisees and Sadducees 'hypocrites' because they failed to understand the teachings of the Old Testament. These men could tell what the weather would be like the next day simply by looking at the sky at night. A red sky at evening meant that a fine day would follow. But they couldn't understand that the Scriptures were being fulfilled before their eyes.

Jesus had done great miracles testifying that he was indeed the promised Messiah. Prophecy had been fulfilled and still the religious leaders of Israel couldn't discern the times. They wanted more signs that would prove that Jesus was who he claimed to be. Jesus told them that the great sign would be that of the prophet Jonah. We read the words of Christ: 'For as Jonah was three days and three nights in the belly of the great fish, so will the Son of Man be three days and three nights in the heart of the earth' (Matthew 12:40).

Reader, do you understand the basic truths of the Bible? If not, if the Bible does not make sense to you, you need God's 'glasses', that is, you need the Holy Spirit to quicken your understanding so that you might understand and believe what God is saying to you in the Scriptures. May God give you a true understanding of his Word.

Activities

1. What makes it possible for a person to understand the teaching of the Bible?
2. What was the greatest sign given by God that Jesus was Messiah?
3. Who is the Holy Spirit?

STORY 16

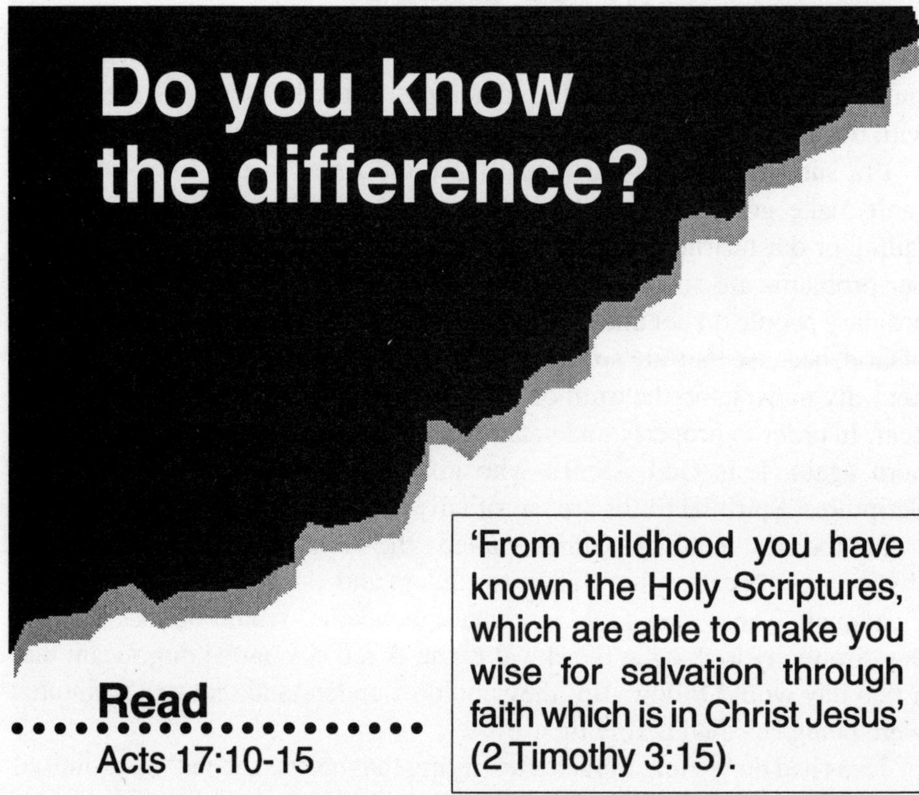

Do you know the difference?

Read

Acts 17:10-15

> 'From childhood you have known the Holy Scriptures, which are able to make you wise for salvation through faith which is in Christ Jesus' (2 Timothy 3:15).

Many non-Christians must be totally confused when they hear the teachings of so many who claim to be Christian teachers. There are so many different groups today who claim to have the truth. Some say, 'If you belong to our church group you will be saved.' Others claim, 'If you live a good life God will allow you to enter heaven.' Some teach that there is no heaven or hell. Others teach that everyone will get to heaven. I remember finding a book in the school library that was called *Many Paths — One Heaven.* The writer of the book taught that no matter what a person believed or did, he or she would one day enter heaven.

It is not only in spiritual matters that we have to make careful choices. When my wife and I visited Thailand some years ago I was tricked into buying what I thought was an ebony elephant, only to find out later that it was a plastic elephant coated with black paint.

Sometimes when you buy a new item — like the computer I'm using now — the warranty says that if you don't use the right parts, the ones supplied by the manufacturer, then the warranty is of no use.

I have already told you several stories about cats our family had as pets. Today I would like to tell you a story about the pet cat at the retirement village where my mother lives. She lives in a unit and has her own car, cooks her own meals and looks after herself. We live only a couple of kilometres from her home so we are able to visit frequently. This is handy for both Mum and myself. Lately doctors and health workers have suggested that pets are very good therapy for people getting on in years. So the management of the home has permitted the people to have some pet cats.

Now imagine the life of a pet cat, when he has about seventy people taking care of him, seventy laps to sit on, seventy people to pat and stroke him, seventy doors to get through and lots of beds to sleep on. Then there are seventy or so people to provide the cat with food. The life of a cat at this retirement home is one of total relaxation and pleasure.

Mum has made a friend of one particular cat. When he sees a light on in her room he comes up and claws at the door, because he knows that he will get a good feed. And when the door is opened, he trots over to the refrigerator and sits there looking at the door. He has learned that milk and meat are stored there. On several occasions Mum has bought him a meal of prawns. Mum always gives him a pat and talks to him.

One morning the cat was at the door and meowing for food. Mum opened the door and said, 'Hello Sammy. How are you today? Would you like some warm milk?'

Sam trotted over to the refrigerator and waited. But on this occasion there was no milk in the fridge. So Mum did the next best thing — she made up some milk using powdered milk. When it was whipped up Mum put it in the microwave and heated it. I think Sammy knows the ring of the microwave means milk. When the milk was warm Mum put it in a bowl and watched as Sammy put his tongue into the made-up mixture.

Mum said you could almost see the look of horror on his face. He could see a white fluid that looked like milk. It was warm like milk. It even smelt like milk, but Sammy knew that it wasn't true milk. He put his nose down again into the powdered milk mixture and then turned and walked out of the room.

Mum just laughed at the hard-to-please Sammy. I imagine he went to someone else's room to get a drink of genuine cow's milk. Sammy could tell the genuine milk from the imitation milk. Nobody could fool him.

Reader, are you like Sammy concerning spiritual matters? Are you able to tell the difference between the true and the false? Sammy knew when something different was being served up.

Our text for today reminds us that the Word of God is able to show us the way of salvation. So each one of you must be a student of the Scriptures, which Peter calls 'the pure milk of the word' (1 Peter 2:2). The more you know of God's Word, the less chance there is that you will be led astray by false teachers.

In the biblical passage for today you will notice that after the Bereans listened to the preaching of Paul and Silas, they went and examined the

Scriptures to make sure that what they heard was indeed the truth. It is the Bible that declares the truth and shows you what is false.

Sammy could tell the difference between real milk and powdered milk. As you get to know the Scriptures God will safeguard you from false teaching. Many false teachers sound and look very attractive. They are sheep in wolves' clothing!

Activities

1. How is it possible for any person to gain entry to heaven?
2. Who is Jesus?
3. Who were the Bereans? Why does the Bible mention them?

STORY 17

Don't be so hard on my friend!

Read

Hebrews 7:20-28

'For there is one God and one Mediator between God and men, the Man Christ Jesus' (1 Timothy 2:5).

I'm sure there are some days that you don't like going to school. Maybe you haven't done your homework, or you don't feel so well. Then there are those days when things happening at home are more exciting than the events at school. One of my granddaughters wanted to stay home one day, but her mother said, 'No'. However, about an hour after school started there was a phone call saying that someone was ill and would her Mum come and collect her? Yes, there are some days when you don't want to go to school!

Have you ever sat in a class with your mother or father as the teacher? I taught each one of my daughters at some stage in their lives. It didn't bother me who was in my class, but there were times when my daughters wished they were not in my class. I always tried to be very fair when teaching a class with my daughter as a member. But so often at the tea table one of the girls would say, 'Dad, you were a bit hard on me today. You aren't that tough on other kids.' Many times I had to apologise, but I didn't want other pupils complaining that I was easy on my own children and hard on others. When someone was in trouble, my own children found it hard as sometimes other children would complain to them about their father.

One day at school, Kim, who was a friend of my daughter Cathie, was in trouble. I remember telling her I was disappointed with her behaviour, and would like to see her the next morning as she would be given some punishment. I think she may have had a sleepless night! That night, at tea time, Cathie spoke up: 'Dad, you were too hard on Kim today. She spoke to me after school and said she wasn't totally to blame. She is really upset and asked me to speak to you before she sees you tomorrow. Please don't be hard on her. She is one of my best friends.'

I thought for a while, as everyone sitting at the table waited to hear what I was going to say. 'All right, Cathie. Because you asked me you can tell Kim not to bother coming to see me tomorrow,' I replied. 'I'll just forget the matter this time.'

The next morning Kim came to me and said, 'Thanks for being so kind, Mr Cromarty.'

Cathie was really the mediator, the go-between, between Kim and myself. And Cathie was the best mediator Kim could find. Cathie was her friend, and Cathie had my ear, because she was my daughter. Maybe Kim thought, 'Mr Cromarty loves Cathie and I'm sure he'll give in to her when she asks on my behalf.' And that was exactly what happened.

Our text for today tells us that Jesus Christ is the only mediator between God and man. The Bible tells us that Jesus Christ is both God and man in one person. This is hard for you (and me) to understand. But because Jesus is both God and man, he is the perfect Mediator.

As a man, Jesus understands our problems. He never experienced actual sin, but he knows what sin can do to a person, because he carried our sins and took the punishment due to us. He knows what it is like to be tired and hungry. There were times when he had no bed to sleep in. He was hated by people and eventually killed by wicked men. Christ's friends deserted him when they were most needed by him. Jesus understands us, because he is truly a man. We can take our problems to him.

But Jesus Christ is also God. The apostle John wrote of Christ, 'In the beginning was the Word, and the Word was with God, and the Word was God' (John 1:1). Because Christ is God he has the ear of God. He is the beloved Son of God and is dearly loved by his Father.

Jesus Christ has done great things on behalf of his people. He paid the penalty for their sins. He won the righteousness his people needed to be saved. Because of this and the Father's great love for his Son, Christ can plead with God on our behalf. And just as I forgave Kim, because my daughter Cathie asked on her behalf, so also God will forgive our sins and grant us blessings, because God loves his Son who saved his people.

Our text tells us that there is only one God. This is true. But let us always remember that there is only one mediator between God and man. When we pray we do so in the name of Jesus Christ, our Saviour, Lord and Mediator. Some would tell us that the saints are mediators, but this is not true. There are many who declare that Mary, the mother of Jesus, is a mediator. But this is also not true. You must believe what the Bible tells you, and our text for today is very clear.

When you pray, pray only in the name of Jesus Christ. From your reading you will know that this very day Jesus is in heaven acting as the Mediator of his people when he speaks to God. Praise God that he has given his people the perfect Mediator — Jesus Christ who is both God and man in one person.

Activities

1. What is a mediator?
2. What is it that makes Christ the perfect and only mediator between God and man?
3. Jesus understands our problems, sorrows and joys. Why is this so?

STORY 18

Beware of the snake!

Read

Romans 1:18-23

'He who believes in Him is not condemned; but he who does not believe is condemned already, because he has not believed in the name of the only begotten Son of God' (John 3:18).

I would like to tell you another true snake story. It happened to the same man, Don, who was mentioned in a story in my first book. I told you that Don had a real liking for snakes. He would never kill a snake and when he was a boy he would usually have one as a pet. He had never been bitten by one but always treated them with care and respect.

Don owned a small property that was covered with trees. He spent a lot of time putting a road into his plot of land. He then began the hard work of clearing the trees from an area where he wanted to plant fruit trees and make a garden. He used a chain-saw to cut the trees down and then dug out the roots with a pick and shovel. It was very hard work, but Don really enjoyed the country life and always had his shirt off, working away.

One day, as he was digging out some tree roots he discovered a very big red-belly black snake. These snakes are poisonous, but their bite doesn't usually kill. However they can make a person very sick. Don quickly grabbed the snake by its tail and walked over to his van, found a bag and dropped the snake in. Then he found a piece of string and tied the top of the bag to prevent the snake escaping. This done, he carefully pushed the bag containing the snake under the rear seat. He had decided to take it to work and show his workmates.

Several days later Don came to see me and there was a worried look on his face.

'What's the matter, Don?' I asked.

'You remember me telling you about the snake I caught and put under the back seat of the car,' Don said. 'Well the bag's still under the seat, but the snake is missing. It must be somewhere in the van. Will you give me a hand looking for it?'

I immediately moved away from the van. I didn't want anything to do with a snake. But I said to Don, 'You go ahead and search for it. I'll just stand here with this shovel and talk to you.'

Don began looking for the snake. He lifted up seats and eventually from under the front seat he pulled out a big black snake. It had escaped from the bag and then curled up in a warm spot in the van. Don dropped the snake back into the bag and then turned to me and said, 'Don't you ever tell anyone about this. I'll never live it down!'

Thinking back, this story teaches us a very important biblical truth. Don and his family were in real danger from the snake that had escaped from the bag. The danger was there and they did not know about it. It was only when Don realized that the snake had escaped, and did something about it, that safety was restored.

Our text reminds us that every person in this world who does not trust in the Lord Jesus Christ is in danger. Many do not know of their dangerous situation because of sin, but that doesn't change the facts. They are guilty before God and, as our text tells us, they are already condemned. It is as if

God has already raised his sword of anger, ready to fall whenever he pleases. Every day that passes is a day wasted if you do not repent of your sins.

Reader, if you are not a Christian do not waste your time! Pray that God will send his Holy Spirit into your heart, that you might become a son or daughter of the living God. The Bible reading for today tells us how foolish people are. The evidence for God is all around them, but they go on living in terrible sin. They don't understand that they are in danger of God's great judgement.

Reader, be wise. If you are not a Christian your sentence is eternal hell. All that has to happen now is for the sentence to be carried out. No one can escape the Judgement Day, but you can escape the judgement of condemnation by trusting in Christ alone for your salvation. May God have mercy upon you.

Activities

1. Why do you think the Bible refers to Satan as the 'serpent'?
2. What does it mean to be 'under God's condemnation'?
3. Who are under God's condemnation?
4. What must be done for God's anger to be removed from a sinner?

STORY 19

A shaking experience

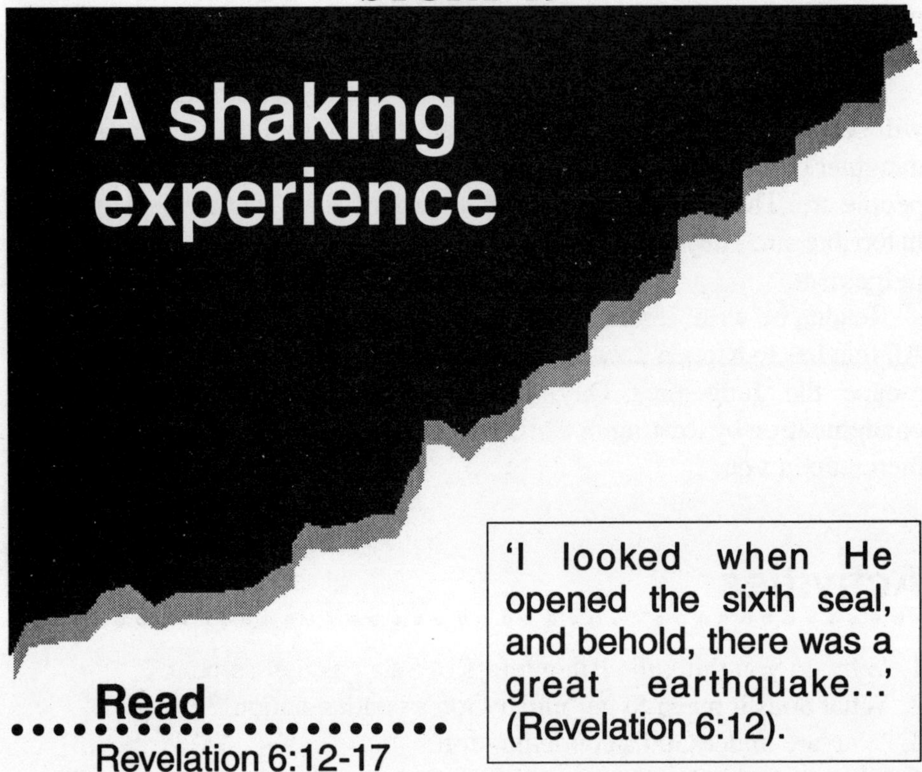

Read

Revelation 6:12-17

> 'I looked when He opened the sixth seal, and behold, there was a great earthquake...' (Revelation 6:12).

In some parts of the world earthquakes are a common experience. I'm sure that to be where there is a great earthquake would be a frightening experience.

Some years ago my wife and I went to a church camp. It was set in the hills to the south of Sydney. It was a wonderful spiritual experience and I urge you to take part in such camps when you have the opportunity. We had lectures, discussion times, singing, prayer times and of course time for talking to friends and enjoying the time together. The area around the camp was covered with trees, but in the distance we could see a clearing and it appeared as if there was a rock quarry. With binoculars I could see trucks coming and going all day.

One day at about midday, we were in the hall listening to a talk when we heard a rumbling sound and suddenly there was what sounded like a huge explosion beside one wall of the building. The whole building shuddered and it seemed as if the thunder passed through the room and out the opposite side. Everyone just looked about them in amazement. Then someone said, 'That was a big explosion! They must be blasting rock out at the quarry.' So the lecture continued.

Before lunchtime as we wandered about the camp grounds someone said, 'I've just heard the news and there's been an earthquake at Newcastle!' Quite a number of the campers came from the Newcastle area and of course wanted to find out about their loved ones and their homes. Telephones were jammed with callers. Finally we heard on the news broadcast that some people had been killed and millions of dollars of damage had been done to buildings. The earthquake was not a large one in comparison to some in other parts of the world. I remember going home to find that the church manse had some cracked walls and it looked as if the whole building had moved about two centimetres across its foundations. One member of the church had his home so extensively damaged that he had to move and buy another home.

The newspapers were filled with pictures and articles about the earthquake and the possible causes. But nowhere did I read that this earthquake, and indeed all earthquakes, came as the judgement of God upon a wicked world and a warning of that great earthquake that heralds the return of Jesus Christ and the judgement that will follow. Despite the deaths and damage done to the city, much space in the local newspapers was devoted to humorous incidents that took place during the earthquake. But it was noticeable that God was missing from all the newspaper reports. No reporter warned the readers that the quake was an indication that God was calling sinners to repent.

In the Bible selection you have for reading today, we have a very descriptive passage depicting the upheavals in the world at the return of Christ. Sin has not only affected every human being in a tragic way, but has had evil consequences for the physical world. Paul wrote, 'We know that the whole creation groans and labours with birth pangs together until now' (Romans 8:22). We also know that following the return of Christ, this world will be renewed. The apostle Peter wrote of the day in 'which the heavens will be dissolved being on fire, and the elements will melt with fervent heat'. He looked forward towards a 'new heavens and a new earth in which righteousness dwells' (2 Peter 3:12-13).

I remember preaching on the Sunday following the earthquake, taking for my text Joel 3:16: 'The LORD also will roar from Zion, and utter His voice from Jerusalem; the heavens and earth will shake; but the LORD will be a shelter for His people, and the strength of the children of Israel.'

I feel sure that many Christian ministers would have done the same. But I have never heard of any person who became a Christian through God's earthquake warning. Every calamity that falls upon mankind is a warning from God of the great judgement that will come. And every calamity is a call from God for people to repent of their sins and trust in Jesus Christ for salvation.

Tens of thousands of people have been killed in some earthquakes, but again the Bible tells us that the final shaking of the earth, at the coming of Christ, will be of greater magnitude than anything before. We read John's words in Revelation 16:18: 'And there were noises and thunderings and lightnings; and there was a great earthquake, such a mighty and great earthquake as had not occurred since men were on the earth.'

There are times when we look up into the sky and see the rainbow. This reminds us that God who once destroyed the world by flood at the time of Noah will not do so again. Every time you hear of an earthquake, remember the return of Christ and the judgement that will follow.

Reader, make sure that you are able to face that judgement with confidence, because you are one of Christ's people.

Activities

1. Give three reasons why earthquakes are frightening.
2. What is God telling people when an earthquake takes place?
3. The Bible tells of an earthquake during the time Jesus was on earth. When was this and what happened at the time of that earthquake?

STORY 20

A faithful horse

'Greater love has no one than this, than to lay down one's life for his friends' (John 15:13).

Read

John 19:1-16

If you have read my stories up to this point you will know that I grew up on a farm. My brother and I have some very happy memories of life on the farm. There were always plenty of jobs to be done, but life was free and easy. We had many pets to play with. There were trees to climb and as our farm was beside a river, we could swim as much as we liked. There was always time for fishing and we had a rowing boat in which we spent many happy hours.

But unlike living in the city, our friends were quite a distance away. We would have to ride our bikes or horses for a kilometre or so to meet our mates for games. This we did quite a lot. In those days there was no television — just the radio. We had to make our own fun. Cricket in summer and football in winter were the games we played in the paddocks. We had a lot of good fun with each other. But most of us spent a good deal of time with horses.

I would like to tell you a true story about one of my young friends and his very faithful horse. Michael had a horse and they were the very best of friends. Michael could catch the horse very easily and he spent a lot of time riding about the paddocks. He would do some jumping on the horse — over logs and drains. One special job he had was to round up the cattle at milking time. His father would go to the milking shed and prepare the dairy for the milking of about eighty cows, while Michael rounded up the cattle on his horse. This was an easy job as the cows were usually ready for the milking and just the appearance of Michael on his horse would mean they started walking towards the dairy.

One evening when Michael had rounded up the herd and they were moving towards the dairy, the bull, for some reason, snorted a few times, kicked some dust over his shoulder, put down his head and charged towards the horse. Michael and the horse were caught unawares and the horse soon had a wound in his side from the horns of the bull.

Michael was thrown to the ground and in his fall broke his leg. The bull turned his attention from the horse, who was bleeding from his side, to Michael, who was lying in agony on the ground. But that horse could see what was going to happen and somehow he knew that he had to protect his young master. The horse raced towards the bull and began to chase him away from Michael. Several times the bull charged at Michael and each time the horse put himself between Michael and the angry bull. The horse was torn again by the bull's horns, but he didn't give up.

Michael began calling out to his father, who heard his cries. When he saw what was happening he sent the dog towards the bull. Dad also raced to Michael's aid.

There was a happy ending to the story. Michael ended up in hospital for a couple of weeks, but his leg healed and there was no pernnanent damage. The veterinary surgeon was able to stitch up the horse's wounds and he was soon well enough to be ridden again. The bull settled down again and never repeated his attack.

But what a faithful horse! He was willing to put his life at risk for a human being. He risked being killed by that angry bull. Surely such an action is a sign of love. I know Michael loved that horse more than ever after that event. The faithful horse had saved his life.

Look at the text for today. Those words were spoken by Jesus and tell a great truth. Isn't it true that the greatest act of love one person can show to another is to die saving that person's life? Would you be willing to die for someone you love? I trust you would. Would you be willing to die for a friend? Maybe you would. Would you be willing to die for someone who hated you? I don't think so!

Jesus Christ died in the place of his people. And Christ did not die for us because we loved him. In fact the Bible tells us the truth about his death and our attitude towards him when he died. Paul wrote, 'But God demonstrates His own love toward us, in that while we were still sinners, Christ died for us' (Romans 5:8).

Think of it! The holy Son of God loved sinners so much that he would die to save them. What a love! And again the Bible tells us that 'We love Him because He first loved us' (1 John 4:19). What a debt of love we owe to our great God and Saviour, Jesus Christ!

Reader, do you love Jesus? Do you show your love to Christ by obedience to his commands? Because of your sins you are under the wrath of God. May it be that you are a true servant of Jesus, filled with his love and protected from his wrath. If you are a Christian, Christ was your sin-bearer. He became sin for you and bore your guilt, shame and punishment. What a wonderful Saviour is Jesus!

Activities

1. What is the greatest expression of love that any person can show to another?
2. How did Jesus show his love of his people?
3. Talk about the ways you can show your love of Christ.

STORY 21

He died all alone

Read
Matthew 27:27-54

'My God, My God, why have You forsaken Me?' (Matthew 27:46).

Loneliness is a terrible feeling. I'm sure that there have been times when you, reader, have been lonely. It may be that someone you thought was a great friend has turned away from you and no longer has anything to do with you. It could be that you are away from home and have no friends. You feel very lonely in such a situation.

I remember the day we took our daughter Heather to the university several hundred kilometres from home and dropped her off so she could begin her studies. Everyone shed tears when we said farewell. She had a comfortable room in the university grounds, but she didn't know anyone. After tea the next night there was a telephone call, reverse charges, and there was Heather, crying and saying, 'I'm so lonely. I want to come home!' But she stayed and made friends and came into contact with the Navigators, a group of Christians who worked amongst the university students. After that there were no more tears and she was no longer lonely.

I'd like to tell you a true and sad story about a lonely old man. I never met this man. I didn't even know he existed, even though he lived only a couple of kilometres from the country school in which I was teaching. For about five years we lived in a schoolhouse in a sheep and wheat area and I was in charge of a two-teacher school. Not so far from the school there was an area set aside for gold prospectors. It was a heavily timbered area and a few people had moved out from town and built themselves shacks in the bush. They didn't have to pay rates, but they had no water or electricity laid on. They had no telephones. They lived a tough, hard life.

Several children from that area attended the school, and often they would bring along small nuggets of gold which they found when they had done some prospecting. I don't think they made much money, but they had a very carefree life.

One morning before school one of the children from the prospecting area ran to our home and asked me to ring for the ambulance, as a man in one of the old shacks was very ill. This I did, and it wasn't long before the ambulance arrived with lights flashing and the young boy jumped in to direct the driver to the sick man.

Within fifteen minutes there was another knock on the door and there stood the ambulance driver. He simply said, 'May I use the phone to ring the police? The old fellow is dead. He's been dead for a day or so.'

Within a short time the police arrived and several hours later the young boy who had raised the alarm arrived at school. Everyone was anxious to know what had happened.

Ross told us the story. A week beforehand he had heard the man call out as he was walking past the shack. Ross went in to find the man on the floor. He was an old man and had fallen out of bed and, as we later found out, had broken his leg. He asked Ross to get him back on his bed. After he had helped the man back to his bed, Ross said he would get the ambulance. However, the man said, 'No, I'll be all right.'

For almost a week Ross took food prepared by his parents to the old man. Ross told us that the night before, the man did not say anything when he took the food into the old hut. I guess he must have been unconscious or even dead at that time. Then the next morning when Ross told his parents that the old man was still asleep they decided to call the ambulance.

That poor old man lived all alone. Most of the locals didn't even know he existed. Some people from the prospecting area used to get food for him. No one knew anything about the man. He died alone and was buried without anyone mourning his passing. How tragic this was!

If we feel lonely we need to go to Christ in prayer and tell him of our loneliness. He understands how we feel, because he experienced a loneliness that we shall never experience. When Jesus was arrested, his friends the disciples deserted him for a time. They feared that they too would be put to death. At the time when Jesus needed his friends the most he found himself alone.

In our Bible reading for today we read of Peter who, when following Christ after his arrest, was accused by a servant girl: 'You also were with Jesus of Galilee.' But we read on, 'But he denied it before them all, saying, "I do not know what you are saying"' (Matthew 26:69-70). In fact the Bible tells us that when a third person accused Peter of knowing Christ, 'He began to curse and swear, saying, "I do not know the Man!"' (v. 74).

But the greatest punishment that Jesus Christ bore for his people was that his fellowship with his Father was broken. God turned his back upon the Sin-bearer for that period of time when he hung upon the cross. Christ suffered our hell upon the cross, and hell is the place of separation from God. It is the place of total loneliness. There upon the cross, bearing the sins of his people, Jesus cried out, 'My God, My God, why have You forsaken Me?' (Matthew 27:46). This was hell for Jesus, our Saviour.

And it is true that Jesus was forsaken by God, so that we who are his people might never be forsaken. When we die, we shall not die alone. Our friends may not be with us. Our loved ones may not be holding our hand, but Jesus has said, 'I will never leave you nor forsake you' (Hebrews 13:5).

This is a wonderful promise, because you who are Christ's people can face death with a confidence that others will never know. It is Jesus who by his Spirit will smooth the pillow on which your dying head rests. It is Jesus who will send his angels (Luke 16:22) to take you home to be with him.

What a wonderful Saviour! He was forsaken so that you and I who love him might never be forsaken. This is a wonderful promise of God, who never breaks his word.

Activities

1. Why did Peter deny that he was a follower of Christ?
2. What are some of the things that make hell so terrible?
3. What were the words of Christ found in Matthew 27:46?
4. What does the Bible mean by the words, 'I will never leave you nor forsake you'? (Hebrews 13:5).

STORY 22

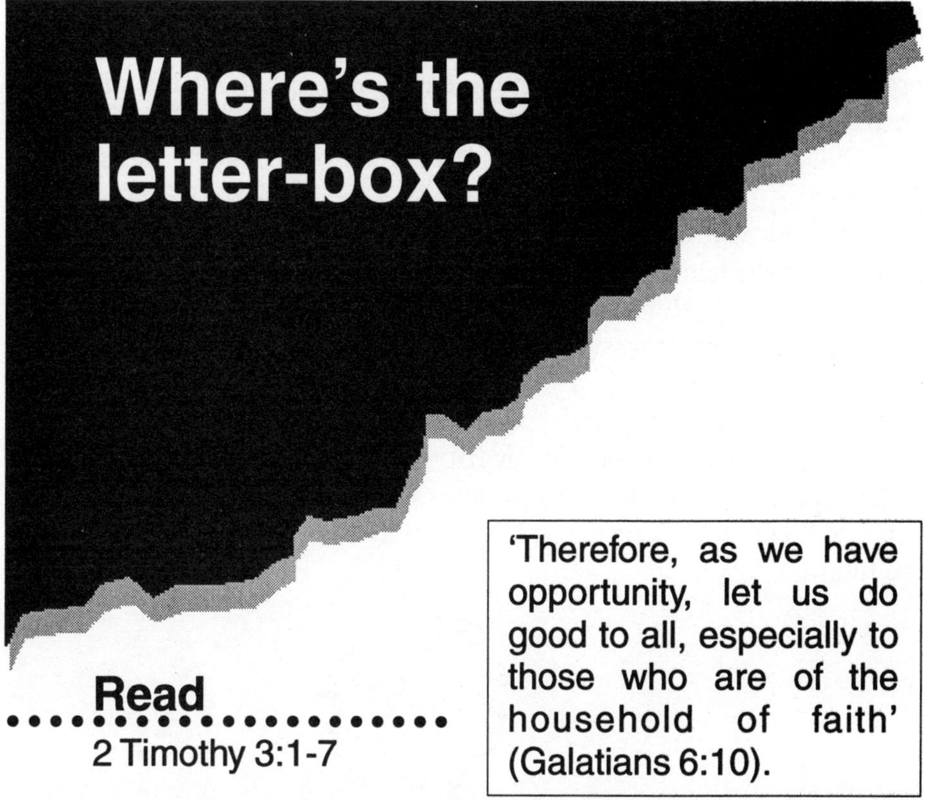

Where's the letter-box?

Read

2 Timothy 3:1-7

'Therefore, as we have opportunity, let us do good to all, especially to those who are of the household of faith' (Galatians 6:10).

Some time ago I was reading a book about the family and copied down several statements found between its covers. I think you'll enjoy reading them.

First I found: 'Our earth is degenerate these latter days; there are signs that the world is speedily coming to an end ... children no longer obey their parents; and the end of the world is surely approaching.'

Then I read, 'I see no hope for the future of our people if they are dependent on the frivolous youth of today, for certainly all youth are reckless beyond words... When I was a boy, we were taught to be discreet and respectful of elders, but the youth of today consider themselves exceedingly wise and oppose all authority.'

And what do you think of these words? 'Children ... show disrespect for elders... Children are now tyrants... They no longer rise when elders enter the room. They contradict their parents, chatter before company ... and tyrannize over their teachers.'

Finally, we are told, 'The young people of today think of nothing but themselves. They have no reverence for parents or old people. They talk as if they alone know everything and what passes for wisdom with us is foolishness to them. As for girls, they are forward, immodest, unwomanly in speech, behaviour and dress.'

If you have read the Bible reading for today, you will find that Paul prophesied of the terrible days at the end of this age. It will be an age of chaos, an age of rebellion against God and man — an age of 'doing your own thing'. It will be an age where the gods of the world are self and pleasure.

Today my wife and I went out into the front garden of our home and noticed that the letter-box was missing from its place on a post. I looked at my wife and said, 'Remember when you heard that noise outside last night and I said I thought it was a cat? Well, there's the result of the noise. Our letter-box is missing.'

'I wonder where it has gone,' said Valerie. 'Have a look over the fence.'

There was the letter-box about fifty metres down the road. Someone had pulled it from its secure position on the post and tossed it away. I suppose if I put it back on the post I shall find it missing again some time in the future.

When I walk along the main street of our town I see some of the young folk who have nothing to do being a nuisance and swearing loudly. Our local newspaper has reports of theft and drunkenness and recently a case of attempted murder. It is not safe to walk along the streets at night-time and my wife and I are having some bars put over windows to prevent the burglars easily getting into our house. So far our house has been broken into twice.

Reader, I imagine you would say that the quotes at the start of this chapter summed up the attitude of quite a few to the young people of this age. However, the first quote was written in about 3000 B.C. by an unknown Assyrian. The second was written by Hesiod at about 700 B.C. The third came from the pen of Socrates, who wrote it in about 400 B.C. The final quote came from Peter the Hermit, who wrote in about A.D.1098. Things haven't changed much, have they?

Reader, take notice of the words of Paul, written to Timothy in today's Bible reading. Do they in any way describe you? There is no doubt that we live in an age of terrible stress. Families are being broken up, nations are at war, there is little respect shown for other people in our society and so many people are interested only in pleasure and themselves.

Our text for today reminds each one of you who professes to be a Christian that you must live a life that is different from that lived by a worldly person. You are to take every opportunity that comes your way to do good to anyone. However, you have a special obligation to do good to your Christian brothers and sisters.

You should not be mixed up with the people who make nuisances of themselves in the street or elsewhere. You should not be like the person who pulled my letter-box off its post and threw it away. You should set an example to the world by Christian living. You must dare to be different from your ungodly friends. By your words and life you should, by the grace of God, do all you can to win them to faith in Christ. You are to love all people — even your enemies. That means you are to do good to those who hate you. In this way you might win them to Christ. Beware of those people who say they are Christians, yet steal and swear and don't live a godly Christian life. Get away from such people, because they can lead you to hell.

And finally, reader, when you are thinking about marriage, make sure you marry a Christian man or woman. I have seen too many Christian people marry non-Christians and end up in a terrible mess spiritually. God has warned us about marrying out of the faith. The Bible tells us that we are 'heirs together of the grace of life' with our marriage partners (1 Peter 3:7).

Activities

1. Whom should Christians marry? Why?
2. Why must Christians live a godly life?
3. What sort of life should young people live?

STORY 23

I don't have a home!

Read

Genesis 12:1-9

> 'These all died in faith, not having received the promises, but having seen them afar off were assured of them, embraced them, and confessed that they were strangers and pilgrims on the earth' (Hebrews 11:13).

In the world today there are millions of people who do not have a home in which to live. If you have a roof over your head, food in your stomach and clothes on your body, you should always give thanks to God for his goodness to you. If you are a Christian you will ever praise God for his gift of salvation of both your soul and body.

Many people live in wealthy countries and yet have no warm, soft bed in which to sleep. We read of many who sleep on the streets, under bridges, in parks and any place where they can find some shelter.

When I was young, tramps (called 'swagmen', or 'swaggies') used to call at our home on the farm, looking for a meal and a place to sleep in return for doing some work. The tramp usually had a dog by his side, and the dog was his best friend. Over his shoulder he carried a bag containing all his earthly possessions. In it he would probably have an old blanket, a spare shirt, maybe some soap, and always some tea, sugar, flour and salt. With these items he could make some 'damper' which is like bread, and of

course he would have a can in which he would boil water and make tea to drink. All the tramps I ever met had cigarettes hanging out of their mouths and they 'rolled their own'. On his head the swagman wore a broad-brimmed hat, with corks hanging on strings around the brim. As the corks bobbed up and down, flies were kept off the man's face.

These men travelled alone and camped here or there, but were always on the lookout for food and tobacco. They used to call at our farm and ask to see Mum. Then they would ask if there was any work they could do in return for food, some money and some tea, sugar and flour. Many times we had dinner with a swagman at the table. Most of them would tell us tales about their adventures as they travelled about Australia.

When we were young it always seemed to my brother and me that these men had a wonderful life. They didn't have to milk cows every day. And I don't think they ever went to school. But now John and I are very pleased we are not swaggies. We both enjoy our warm beds at night-time! But the swaggies didn't have any permanent home. Sometimes they would spend a few days in the hayshed, doing a few odd jobs and having a rest before they set out on their next walk.

Some of them, if they were given a meal and treated well at a particular home, would put a stone on a fence-post, to indicate to other swaggies that the home nearby was a good place for a meal. But it is sad to think of people who have no home or material security in the world.

In our text for today we read of a biblical pilgrim, Abraham, who truly was a pilgrim on this earth. And our Bible reading tells us of God calling Abraham (Abram) to pack up his belongings and leave the security of his home in Ur. God had chosen Abraham to be the father of a people who would be special to God. Abraham obeyed God and travelled to the land of Canaan. We also learn from our reading that God told Abraham that the land of Canaan would one day belong to his descendants (v. 7).

Abraham's obedience to God's command was a great act of faith. Abraham trusted in the Lord and did as he was told. Abraham was one of the ancestors of the Lord Jesus Christ. And he was a pilgrim on the earth. He lived in tents and moved from place to place. The promise of the land was given, but he never owned that land. In fact when his wife Sarah died he owned no plot of land in which to bury her. He had to approach local landowners to purchase the Cave of Machpelah and the surrounding area to use as a cemetery (Genesis 23).

Even though Abraham owned no land, he knew God would fulfil his promise of giving the land of Canaan to his descendants. But more than anything else Abraham and all of God's people longed for the heavenly home which is promised to all who love God and have faith in Jesus Christ.

Abraham and all of God's people are pilgrims on this earth. If you are a Christian the earth is not your home! You are just passing through. Your eternal home is the new heavens and the new earth — the land of righteousness where we shall see the Lord Jesus Christ face to face.

There are so many problems in this world. God's people shed many tears because of sin and the actions of others. May all my Christian readers think more and more about heaven. Think about the wonder and glory that lie before you in your permanent home where God dwells in a very special way. When you think this way, the things of the world will not be the most important things in your life.

Activities

1. In what country was Abraham born?
2. Why did he leave his homeland?
3. In what way are Christians pilgrims in this world?
4. Describe the true home of God's people.

STORY 24

A red moon and a black sun

Read

Joel 2:28-32

> 'I looked when He opened the sixth seal, and behold, there was a great earthquake; and the sun became black as sackcloth of hair, and the moon became like blood' (Revelation 6:12).

Many parts of the world suffer from great droughts. I have known children who first saw rain fall from heaven when they were five years old. This is hard to believe, but it is true.

On the farm we had long periods without rain, but we could water the crops and so survive the droughts. Our greatest problem was the floods that came, sometimes every year. But in the central areas of Australia some of the droughts are very severe. The crops die and the land is just bare dirt. The farmers and graziers in many cases have to sell their cattle, and sometimes they are forced to shoot their starving stock. This is a real tragedy.

Another problem that is associated with drought is the hot winds that blow. Sometimes there are dust storms so thick that you can't see anything at all. People just move into their homes, block up all the cracks and wait for the storm to pass. But the fine dust gets through the smallest spaces and soon there is a sheet of dust over everything in the house. The dust storms can be very frightening.

Many years ago, when I was attending primary school with my brother, there was a dust storm that I can still remember. The dust was blown hundreds of kilometres from the western area of New South Wales. We could see the dust coming over the horizon. It was like huge red clouds filling the sky. Before we went to bed, I can still remember Mum and Dad putting towels at the bottom of the doors to prevent the dust blowing into the house. My brother John and I found it very exciting. We couldn't wait for the morning to see what the sky looked like.

The next morning, we looked up into the heavens and could see red dust everywhere. The wind was blowing and the dust swirled around the house and the trees. We could see about us for only several hundred metres. Looking up into the sky the sun was very dark and the setting moon was a reddish colour. The scene was frightening to John and me. We suggested to Mum and Dad that we should stay home from school that day, but it wasn't long before we were on our bikes, riding down the road towards the town where the school was to be found.

As we rode along John said, 'Isn't it frightening!? Do you remember that part of the Bible where it says that the moon and sun will be red and dark in the sky just before Jesus comes again?'

John and I attended Sunday School and church, and we at times read our Bibles, even though we were not Christians. We knew the passage that is our Bible reading for today. As we continued our long ride to school, we talked about the coming of Christ. In fact I can still remember us wondering if we would get home from school that day. The sky seemed to be telling us both that the second coming of Jesus was just a short time away. We were a bit excited, but also very worried. We didn't at that age know what would happen to us.

Well, we arrived home from school, and had to help with the milking. That night the moon looked very strange, and the next morning the red dust made everything look eerie. But several days later the dust was gone, and Jesus had not returned.

However, the wonderful truth of the Scripture is that one day Jesus Christ, my Lord and my Saviour — and I hope, your Lord and your Saviour — will come again. No one knows the day or the hour — this is known to God alone. Many people have tried to predict the time of Christ's return, but all have failed. As you read your Bibles you will find there some indications of what the world will be like just before it happens. The important thing is for you to be ready to face Christ when he returns — or to face him when you die. The only way you will be able to face Christ, with a smile on your face and joy in your heart, will be if you are trusting in him alone for your salvation.

It will be a great day when Jesus comes again. We shall be given wonderful new bodies that will never wear out or die. We shall meet again our Christian friends and relations who have died in Christ. We shall meet the great saints spoken of in the Bible.

But best of all is that we shall see Jesus Christ, face to face. May God be pleased to bless everyone who reads this book.

Activities

1. What great event will bring the history of this world to an end?
2. When will Christ return to this earth?
3. Are you looking forward to the return of Christ? Why do you say that?

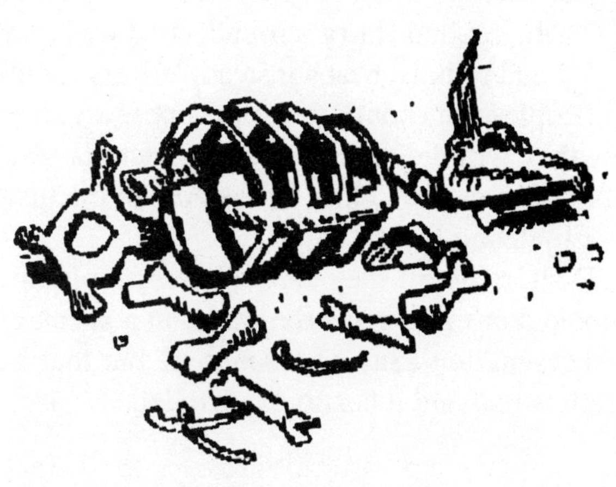

STORY 25

One day I will die

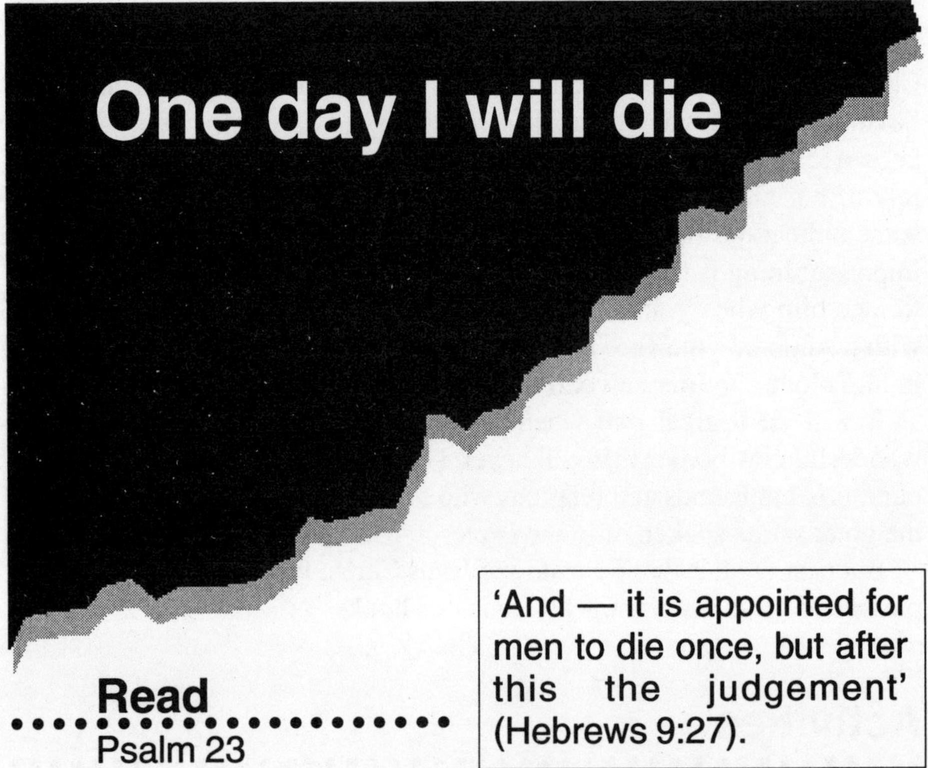

Read

Psalm 23

'And — it is appointed for men to die once, but after this the judgement' (Hebrews 9:27).

People don't like speaking about death. Some time ago I met a particular man who didn't want to talk seriously about death.

He said to me, 'Did you hear the joke about the man who called on his friend to see how he was? When he was met by his friend's wife he asked about Harry. Harry's wife replied, "Harry died last week. We decided to have some fresh green peas from our garden for tea and Harry went down to pick them. He just dropped dead beside the garden."

'"Oh,"replied Harry's friend, "that was terrible. Whatever did you do?"

'"I had to have beans instead," Harry's wife replied.'

People joke about death, but very few people face up to the fact that one day they will die. Every person alive today will die, unless the Lord Jesus Christ comes first. Only two people in the history of the world did not die — Elijah and Enoch.

Doctors do all they can to keep people alive, but in the end they die. People don't like using the words that speak of death. They call a coffin a casket and don't say a person died, but that he or she 'passed away'. But death is real and it cannot be avoided. What then is death?

Well, death is the result of sin and is the separation of the soul from the body. When Adam sinned God said to him, 'For dust you are, and to dust you shall return' (Genesis 3:19). Death for all humans is the ending of all the bodily functions. It is when the soul leaves the body. The soul returns to God for judgement and is either condemned to hell or enters heaven — the presence of God. The body returns to the dust of the earth.

A man named John Quincey Adams was once asked how he was keeping. To this question he replied, 'Thank you, John Quincey Adams is very well himself, sir; but the house in which he lives is falling to pieces. Time and seasons have nearly destroyed it. The roof is well worn, the walls shattered. It trembles with every gale. I think John Quincey Adams will soon have to move out. But he himself is very well, sir.' When John Quincey Adam's body was worn out, his heart stopped beating, he stopped breathing and he himself returned to God, leaving his body behind.

Someone asked me what death was really like, but as I haven't died I couldn't tell from personal experience. But I told the person that at one point in my life I became very ill. The doctors weren't sure what was wrong with me, until one doctor did a special blood test and found I had a tumour on the parathyroid gland. I didn't even know at that time that I had a parathyroid gland. I was transferred from a country hospital to a city hospital for neck surgery.

I remember being taken to the operating theatre and I was so ill. I had pains everywhere. I was sick in the stomach, I couldn't see properly — I was really ill. I had been told that the surgeon would cut my throat open and remove the tumour and then I would be well again. The last thing I remember before the surgery was lying on a very cold bed, in a cold room, surrounded by doctors and nurses sticking a needle into my arm, with a bright light shining into my eyes. I felt very ill and the doctor said to me, 'Soon you'll be asleep. When you wake up you'll feel much better. Try counting to ten.'

I opened my mouth to say, 'One,' but I couldn't say anything.

When I woke up I was in a lovely warm room. The bed was soft and warm. One nurse was sitting beside me. All my aches and pains were gone and even though I felt sleepy I knew I was getting better. I hadn't experienced anything between the last thing I remembered in the operating theatre and waking up in a different room.

Death is something like that. It is like going to sleep on earth and waking up somewhere else. For the Christian it will mean waking up in heaven, in the presence of Christ. God will watch over his people in their death. Jesus has promised that he will never leave his people to suffer alone. All of God's people have been promised the grace to face death with confidence. You may worry about how you will cope with death. But if you are a Christian you will cope very well with dying. You don't need the grace of God to die today, but when death comes God will give you all the courage and strength you need. If you are prepared to die, then you don't have to worry about dying, for death is the gateway to heaven.

Death is an enemy, because God did not create Adam and Eve to die. When they sinned death entered the world. But the Bible tells us very plainly that when Christ returns death will be defeated (read 1 Corinthians 15:50-57). Jesus defeated death when he rose from the grave. And in the kingdom he has prepared for his people, there is no more death, because in that land there is no sin.

Reader, are you ready for the day of your death? You don't know when that day will be, but you know that today is the day when you should make your preparations. The only preparation that is worthwhile is to ask the Lord Jesus Christ to be your Saviour and then trust in him.

Activities

1. Why do people die?
2. When will our enemy death be finally overthrown?
3. What is the best way that you can prepare for your death?

STORY 26

The old flood-house

Read
Matthew 7:21-29

'Not everyone who says to Me, "Lord, Lord," shall enter the kingdom of heaven, but he who does the will of My Father in heaven' (Matthew 7:21).

When you were young I'm sure you liked to have a playhouse (in Australia we call this a 'cubby house'). Several of my grandchildren have cubby houses in their back yards and they seem to have the time of their life. Scott and Jessica have a cubby house built up on stilts. Somewhere Scott found an old Australian flag that now flutters from a mast over the cubby house. In some ways it reminds me of a lookout on a fort in Indian country.

When I was young we had a cubby house and my brother and I used to spend many happy hours in it. I'm sure it was better than any playhouse my readers might have had. I'd like to tell you about it.

Before John and I were born the family lived in a home built beside the river. In those days a lot of travel was done along the river. A milk boat used to come up the river daily to collect the cans of milk. The dairy was also beside the river. But floods were always a problem and many times the flood-water would almost cover the house. My grandparents then built a small wooden flood-house.

It was built on four long poles high above ground level. When a flood came Grandfather would take the cows to higher ground and Grandma would move the precious belongings out of the house and up into the

flood-house. The one-room flood-house was large enough for a stove, a table and chairs and several bunks for sleeping. All this happened before I was born.

But during one flood a large tree trunk smashed into the flood-house and it was a miracle that the whole structure didn't collapse into the river. Grandfather then set to work and moved the flood-house into a huge fig-tree. It was the same building, but in places was securely attached to the fig-tree whose huge spreading branches protected it from all the bits and pieces that were washed down the river in the time of flood. When cars became the means of travel and the milk trucks took over from the boats, the family home was rebuilt beside the road. But the flood-house remained.

In our young days, John and I used the flood-house to play in. We would climb up the ladder and then pull it up so that no one could get in to us. We would light the fire in the old iron stove and make tea to drink. Some nights we stayed in the flood-house, using an old kerosene lantern for light. It was all good fun. Some of Mum and Dad's fishing friends used to come and use the flood-house as a camp while they tried to catch the 'big ones'.

A couple of years ago my wife and I drove past the old farm where I grew up. The house is gone. The dairy is no more — but when I looked across the paddock towards the river I could see the old flood-house, still there, nestled between the branches of that great old fig tree. The flood-house has stood the test of time — I guess it has been there for ninety years or so.

Jesus told a parable about the foolish man who built his house on the sand. That man probably built his house on a dry river-bed. When the rains and flood came it was washed away. This was a little bit like the first flood-house that my grandparents built.

The wise man built his house on a rock that provided security in the day of rain and flood. This was a little bit like the second flood-house my grandparents built. The fig-tree to which it was securely attached was huge. Its roots were deep into the earth and its branches protected the flood-house from the raging flood-waters.

In the parable that we read today Jesus is teaching us a great truth which we need to take to heart. Our text for the day is a summary of the teaching

of that parable. Jesus is telling all who listen to him that it is not enough to simply say, 'I believe in Jesus', and then think that they are saved. I could teach a parrot to say that and his words would mean nothing at all. A Christian is a person who not only says that he follows Jesus Christ, but willingly obeys Christ's commandments. He or she is not just a person who hears, but a person who does what he hears.

The person who simply talks about his faith will not survive the difficult spiritual day. His faith is not a saving faith and it will let him down when it should support him. He is like the foolish man who built his house on the sand.

The true Christian is the person who puts into practice the law of God, because he or she loves God. When the hard times come to this person, his or her faith will stand firm, because it is a living faith. True faith costs the believer much in the world. Such a person turns away from the pleasures of sin to find pleasure in serving the living God. The true believer will sacrifice time and money to glorify Christ. Someone once said, 'A faith that costs nothing is worth nothing!' Another person said, 'There is no gain without pain!'

Reader, is your faith a living faith that will stand the test of daily living so that Christ is glorified? Is your faith in Christ one that will hold you secure on the Day of Judgement?

Activities

1. What is a cubby house? If you have one describe it.
2. Describe the person who built his house on the rock.
3. Read James 2:26 and tell the person with you what it means.

STORY 27

Treasure in the Scriptures!

Read

Psalm 119:97-104
and Matthew 13:44-46

'Therefore I love Your commandments more than gold, yes, than fine gold!' (Psalm 119:127).

We all have treasures — things that mean a lot to us. Usually we take great care of these items and make sure they do not get lost or stolen.

My brother John is a keen gold prospector when he has the time. He has some gold which he has found, but doesn't keep it in his home, but rather in the bank in a safe-deposit box.

The most precious thing in the world is our God and the salvation he has provided through his Son Jesus Christ.

I would like to tell you a story about a very valuable Bible. Several generations ago the settlers in Australia found life on the farms very hard. There was always plenty of work to be carried out clearing the land and ploughing the fields with horse and plough. There were no tractors. Only once in a while were families able to get to town, and money was always in short supply. Many people had just one pair of shoes and these they wore on Sundays, when they attended church. During the week they usually walked about barefoot. Also, banks were few and far between and most country people had to hide their valuables and money well out of the way.

One particular family found life quite hard on the farm. The head of the family was a tough man and made sure his sons worked hard. He didn't give them pay for their work, but they had plenty to eat and their father bought them clothes when he thought they needed them. When they went to town Dad would give the family just enough money to buy what was absolutely necessary.

They had a large family Bible and Dad would not let anyone touch that Bible. It was his alone. It stood on a shelf high above the floor, where children who did not know better could not get at it. Even his wife was not permitted to touch his Bible.

Every now and again the father of the house would take his Bible from the shelf, go alone into a room and spend time with his Bible. The family always thought that Dad was reading God's Word. After several hours alone Dad would return from his room and put the Bible back on the shelf, and again warn the family that no one was to touch it. And they didn't, because they were afraid of what Dad would do if they disobeyed him.

I was told by a grandson that one day he walked into the house and found that everyone was out. He had seen the Bible on the shelf many times and took the opportunity of taking it down and opening its pages. To his surprise he found that between the pages of the Bible there was money. The Bible was used by the old grandfather as a hiding-place for his money. There were notes worth hundreds of pounds here and there between the pages. The grandson quietly put the Bible back and didn't say anything to anyone. He didn't want his grandfather to find out that he had looked where he was told not to look.

The grandson, now a middle-aged man, told me it was then he realized that his grandfather was not reading the Bible when he took it into his room, but was probably counting his money to make sure it was all there. I suppose that the old man thought that if a burglar broke into his home they would never look in a Bible to find any treasure. His money would be safe there between the pages of the Scriptures. When the old man died the family found that the Bible was worth a lot of money. The Bible was the old man's bank.

In the reading for today you should have realized that God's Word is very precious. It is precious because it is the Word of the living God and it is precious because it tells us of the great salvation found in the Lord Jesus Christ. Salvation is so precious that we should be willing to do anything and sacrifice everything to gain that salvation.

Christ told a very short parable about the man who was working in the fields of another man. There he found a treasure hidden in the ground. In those days a container hidden in the ground was as safe as a bank. I imagine the hidden treasure belonged to someone who had died and not told anyone about it. The man who discovered the treasure in the field did not steal it, but sold all he had in order to have enough money to buy the field and so get the treasure for himself.

Jesus is telling you that there is a treasure of immense value, which is salvation through faith in himself. As far as you are concerned that treasure is hidden in the Bible. You must open your Bible and search through its precious pages to find out about yourself and your need of a Saviour. You must be willing to sacrifice all you have to gain that salvation, freely available through faith in Christ.

King David said of God's words, 'How sweet are Your words to my taste, sweeter than honey to my mouth!' (Psalm 119:103). He also wrote, 'Therefore I love Your commandments more than gold, yes, than fine gold!' (Psalm 119:127).

Have you found that treasure which is more valuable than anything that this world can offer? Any sacrifice you are called to make in order to gain Christ is worthwhile. The apostle Paul said of the preciousness of salvation in Christ: 'But indeed I also count all things loss for the excellence of the knowledge of Christ Jesus my Lord, for whom I have suffered the loss of all things, and count them as rubbish, that I may gain Christ and be found in Him...' (Philippians 3:8-9). May you be able to say the same!

Activities

1. Why can Christians say there is treasure in the Scriptures?
2. List three treasures that God has in store for his people?
3. Name three things you treasure that you would be willing to sacrifice for following Jesus Christ.

STORY 28

Confessing Christ

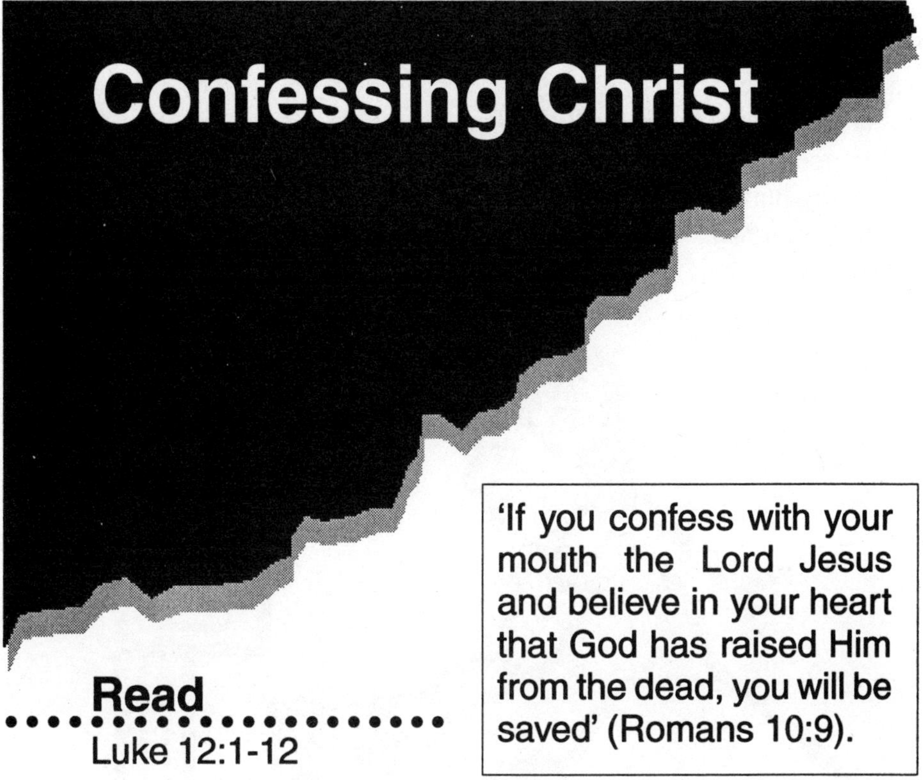

Read

Luke 12:1-12

'If you confess with your mouth the Lord Jesus and believe in your heart that God has raised Him from the dead, you will be saved' (Romans 10:9).

The Bible tells us very plainly that all of God's people are to confess to the world about them that they are Christians — that they love and serve the Lord Jesus Christ. People should recognize that we are Christians just by watching us each day, for we should always do those things that please our Saviour. We should ever be joyful to confess our love for Christ, because he loves us and saved us.

When our children were young we went for a holiday to friends who lived out in the country. It was very cold weather and each morning there would be a thick frost on the ground. I didn't like getting out of bed too early and enjoyed the warmth of the electric blanket. But the girls used to be out of bed before the sun came up. I don't think they felt the cold. We would tell them to put on a warm cardigan, but with all the racing about they somehow kept warm. Now my daughter Vicki tells me that cardigans are those things that children wear when their mothers are cold.

To keep the kitchen warm there was a large open fire kept burning day and night. One morning when my wife and I were thinking about getting out of bed, we heard our daughter Heather, who was five years old, scream very loudly. It sounded as if something terrible was happening to her. We leaped out of bed and ran to the kitchen and there stood Heather in her underwear. In front of her stood Maureen, our friend, and she had Heather's nightie in her hands. Tears were streaming down Heather's frightened face.

'Whatever has happened?' I asked.

Maureen held up Heather's nightie and we could see where the bottom was badly burned. Heather had been standing very close to the open fire and the draught of air going up the chimney had dragged her nightie into the flames.

Maureen had been in the room and seen what was happening. She simply ran towards Heather and with one swift movement lifted the nightie over her head and smothered the flames. Heather had not realized that her nightie was burning and I imagine she didn't know what was happening when Maureen ripped off her nightie. There wasn't a sign of even a hair on her leg being scorched. She had been saved from some terrible burns.

From that day onwards, Heather has been a very good friend of Maureen. She told everyone about the incident and how Maureen had saved her life. Whenever she saw Maureen she would throw her arms about her. It didn't matter where she was — she was never ashamed to let people know that she loved the lady who had saved her from getting badly burnt.

If you are a Christian, you must realize what a great salvation was accomplished by the Lord Jesus Christ. You must have some idea of the great debt of gratitude you owe to the Son of God, who loved you and gave himself for you.

The text for today tells you that if you belong to Christ, you are to confess him day by day to those people with whom you come into contact. You should never be ashamed of Jesus and what he has done for you. Jesus spoke some great words of comfort for all who trust in him alone for salvation. In Matthew 10:32-33 we read, 'Therefore whoever confesses Me before men, him I will also confess before My Father who is in heaven. But whoever denies Me before men, him I will also deny before My Father who is in heaven.'

Imagine if a day came when Heather was ashamed to be seen with Maureen — ashamed to be seen with the person who had saved her from a terrible burning. That would be a disgrace! So also you must never be ashamed of Jesus and what he has done for you. In your reading for today, Jesus tells you that if you confess him before men, he will confess you before the angels in heaven. On Judgement Day Jesus will tell the assembled universe that you belong to him.

How are you to confess Jesus? Well, first of all, you can tell people of God's goodness to you. They may not understand what you are talking about, and may laugh at you, but your love for Jesus and his love for you should never make you ashamed of confessing him. You confess Jesus by living as he would have you live. You confess Christ, by not getting involved with swearing and telling jokes that are disgusting. You confess Christ every Sunday, when you worship him with God's people.

There are just so many ways to let the world know about Christ and his salvation. When my brother and I used to fish out on the ocean, we would take several bottles containing tracts. They were very well sealed. We would throw them overboard. Maybe someone found them and through reading the tracts was led to Jesus.

Oh, reader, you make sure that you confess Jesus to the world in which you live!

Activities

1. How can you confess Christ to the world?
2. What promise has Christ given to all people who confess him before the world?
3. Why do you love Jesus?

STORY 29

Jesus Christ — the God-man

Read

Philippians 2:5-11

'But when the fulness of the time had come, God sent forth His Son, born of a woman...' (Galatians 4:4).

Most parents look forward to the birth of a baby. I know that my wife and I did. The first child in our family was a daughter. We had been married several years and when a baby was on the way we were very excited. We made all the necessary preparations. There was a room for the new baby and my wife had bought all the clothes and bits and pieces that were needed to help cope with the new arrival. But I had no real idea what to expect. I can still remember taking my wife to the hospital and being told by the nurses to say 'Goodbye'. I left Valerie and went to school, teaching all day, but ringing the hospital every now and again to find out how things were going.

The baby was born, and ten days later our baby girl was taken home. That was the first time I was able to have a good look at my daughter. In those days, fathers went to the hospital and were able to look through a glass window at the rows of babies. A nurse would lift your baby out of its cradle and bring it to the window. All a father could do was look through the glass and long to hold the little one in his arms.

But at home it was all different. I could touch the baby and nurse her. However, the first night with the baby at home was a disaster. She cried

and cried. Valerie got out of bed and fed her and then tried to settle her down to sleep. I didn't get much sleep and was very tired when I went to school the next day. This problem went on for weeks and I eventually slept in the room the greatest distance from the baby, in order to get a rest. I began to wonder why babies are called 'bundles of joy'.

We have a wonderful Saviour who is both God and man in the one person. Our text and reading for today tell us very clearly that Jesus Christ the Son of God was a true man as well as being God. Jesus, our Redeemer, was no ordinary baby.

When he was born he must have looked like any other baby. He would have cried when he needed food. Mary, his mother, would have fed him on her breast and done all the things mothers have to do with babies. Jesus had to be a true human in order to die in the place of his people. The great difference between the humanity of Jesus and you and me is that he was born without sin and never sinned. But he was tempted to sin and so understands what we go through when Satan and his demons tempt us.

Christ didn't come into the world to save the sinful angels, but sinful humans. In Hebrews 2:14-18 we read, 'Inasmuch then as the children have partaken of flesh and blood, He Himself likewise shared in the same, that through death He might destroy him who had the power of death, that is, the devil, and release those who through fear of death were all their lifetime subject to bondage. For indeed He does not give aid to angels, but He does give aid to the seed of Abraham. Therefore, in all things He had to be made like His brethren, that He might be a merciful and faithful High Priest in things pertaining to God, to make propitiation for the sins of the people. For in that He Himself has suffered, being tempted, He is able to aid those who are tempted.'

Jesus truly was man, but he also was God. Paul said of Christ, 'For in Him dwells all the fulness of the Godhead bodily' (Colossians 2:9). And the apostle John said of Christ, the Word of God, 'In the beginning was the Word, and the Word was with God, and the Word was God' (John 1:1).

An angel spoke to Joseph, the husband of Mary, and told him of the baby that was to be born to his wife. Joseph was not Christ's father, but Jesus' conception was a miracle for he had no human father. The angel said, '"Behold a virgin shall be with child, and bear a Son, and they shall call His name Immanuel," which is translated, "God with us"' (Matthew 1:23).

I can't understand how Jesus Christ can be both God and man in one person, but the Bible tells me this and so I believe God's Word. This is a true mystery, but I look at myself in the mirror and see that I am made up of two great parts — body and soul. My body can die, but I still live. Two parts, yet one person! I think I'm a mystery too. And so are you!

And so Jesus came into the world to save his people. He couldn't save us by remaining in heaven. He had to come into this world as a man and die upon a cross, so that sinners might be saved.

A schoolteacher I knew many years ago went to a cliff overlooking the ocean one Friday afternoon. As he stood up to go home, the stones on which he was standing slipped and he fell about forty metres to the rocks below. He broke both of his legs and had some terrible injuries. He lived alone and no one knew that he was missing. Two days later some people heard him calling for help. The police arrived with the cliff rescue squad and looked down at David. To save him, it was necessary for one policeman to be lowered over the cliff so that he could get down to where he lay. Had the rescue squad remained at the top of the cliff, David would have died.

David was saved, and taken to a very large hospital where he was treated for several months. He walks with a limp today and is very careful when he looks over a cliff. He was saved by the men who came down to him.

Jesus Christ, the God-man, did the same. He came into this world of sin and trouble as a true man to save men and women. He came into this world as truly God that he might provide a worthy sacrifice for sin. As God he could present his sacrifice to his Father. This you and I could never do, because we are sinners.

Read these wonderful words of Psalm 40: 1-2: 'I waited patiently for the LORD; and He inclined to me, and heard my cry. He also brought me up

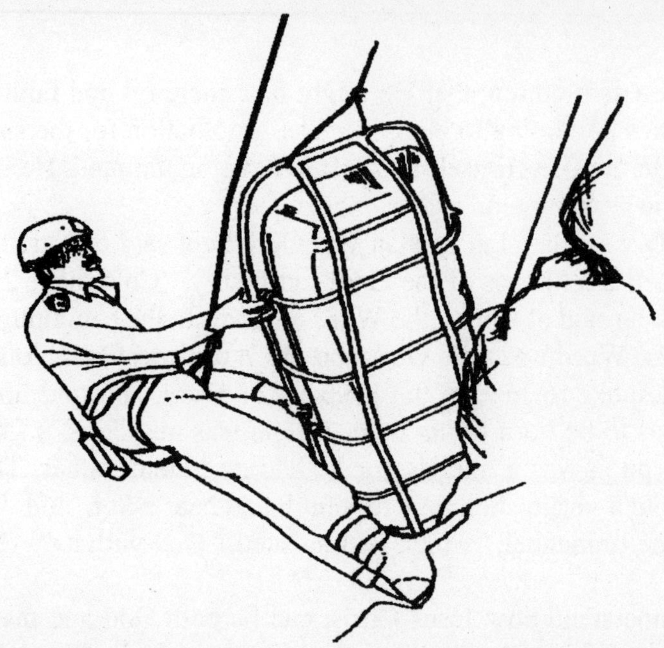

out of a horrible pit, out of the miry clay, and set my feet upon a rock, and established my steps.' Jesus did this for all of his people.

Activities

1. What sort of a young lady was the mother of Jesus?
2. In what way was Jesus different from ordinary men and women?
3. What is meant by the teaching that Jesus was the God-man?
4. Why was it necessary for Jesus to come into the world as the God-man?

STORY 30

A forgetful God

Read

Luke 7:36-50

'I will forgive their iniquity, and their sin I will remember no more' (Jeremiah 31:34).

Holidays are great! There are three things about holidays that I truly enjoy.

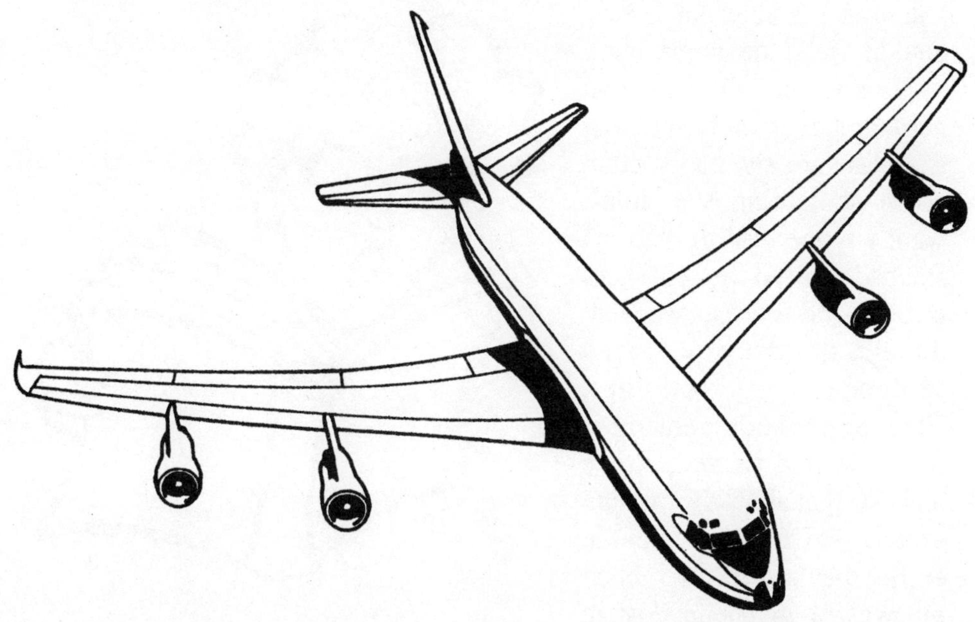

First of all, there is the fun preparing for the holiday. There is the looking at maps and wondering what things will be like. I know my wife always looks forward to any trip we might have on an aeroplane. I don't like that part of holidays as I like to have my feet planted firmly on the ground. When we visited Hong Kong we planned what we hoped to do. We wrote to the Hong Kong Travel Bureau and were sent brochures about places to visit. There is always fun preparing for holidays.

Secondly, and the best part of the holiday, is the actual holiday. To really see the places you have planned to see can be very exciting. Most people take photographs of important events and places, and that gives you something else to enjoy about your holiday.

Thirdly, when you get home, you can take out the photos and show them to people, telling them all about the good time you had. Every now and again I take out the photographs of holidays we have had as a family. I sit down and look at the scenes. Just sitting and looking brings back pleasant memories.

Now you may ask, how can this have anything to do with a forgetful God, which is the subject of today's text and Bible reading? Well, one day I took out our photographs of the holiday we had in Hong Kong and my wife Valerie said, 'I think I kept a diary when we visited Hong Kong. I wonder where it is?'

Valerie then jumped up and began looking for her diary. Soon she found it and we sat down together to read it as we looked at the photographs. It was great to talk about the good time we had in Hong Kong. However as we turned a page of the diary we found that some sentences had been scrubbed out and we couldn't read the words at all.

Valerie thought long and hard, and eventually said that she was sure she had written down something she didn't want anyone else to read, so she had crossed the sentences out. Several times as we went through the diary we found sentences scrubbed out. Valerie couldn't remember what she had written, so we had to forget about the missing sentences. I'm sure one of the entries that had been scrubbed out was of my being lost in

Macau, which I wrote about in an earlier story. But the diary was a record of the good time we had.

Do you know that God has kept and is still keeping a 'diary' of your life on earth? In that diary is every thing you have done and every thought that has passed through your mind. But not only that, every word you have spoken is recorded in God's diary of your life. We read passages of God's Word that tell us this frightening truth. For example in Revelation 20:12 we have the scene of the great Day of Judgement and we read, 'And I saw the dead, small and great, standing before God, and books were opened. And another book was opened, which is the Book of Life. And the dead were judged according to their works, by the things which were written in the books.' Everything you have ever done has been recorded.

How do you think you will feel when Jesus Christ, the great Judge, calls out your name and there you stand before the watching universe, and the books are opened? Could it be that when Jesus Christ turns the pages he finds certain things scrubbed out so that no one can read them?

Reader, if you are a Christian, God will not parade your sins before a watching world, because as our text for today says, 'I will forgive their iniquity, and their sin I will remember no more.' This same truth is taught throughout the Scriptures. Listen to these words: 'You will cast all our sins into the depths of the sea' (Micah 7:19). And what about this passage: 'As far as the east is from the west, so far has He removed our transgressions from us'? (Psalm 103:12). If you look at your atlas you will find that north and south have fixed points, the north and the south pole, but east and west are in opposite directions and have no fixed points. In other words, God has removed the sins of his people and they will be gone for ever.

It is wonderful to know that the blood of Jesus Christ does indeed cleanse us from all of our sins (1 John 1:7). The sins of Christ's people have been forgiven and God has forgotten them. On Judgement Day, if you are a Christian, none of your sins will be dragged up before you to condemn you. Jesus Christ, the great Judge, will sit there upon his throne of judgement as your Saviour. He will welcome you into the eternal home he has prepared for his people.

In the Bible reading for today we read of a wicked woman who came to Christ, weeping over her terrible sins. She confessed her sins to Jesus and he said to her, 'Your sins are forgiven' (Luke 7:48). Has Jesus said this to you? You cannot hear him speak, but you can read his promise that if you confess your sins he will forgive you (1 John 1:9). His promise is good enough for me! God has forgiven my sins and forgotten them. It is wonderful that we do have a forgetful God in this matter.

Activities

1. Why should God forgive the sins of anyone?
2. God forgives his people's sins. What does this mean?
3. Learn the words of 1 John 1:7.

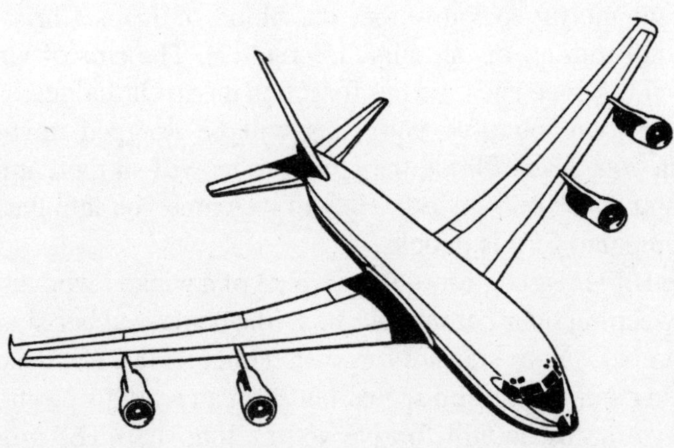

STORY 31

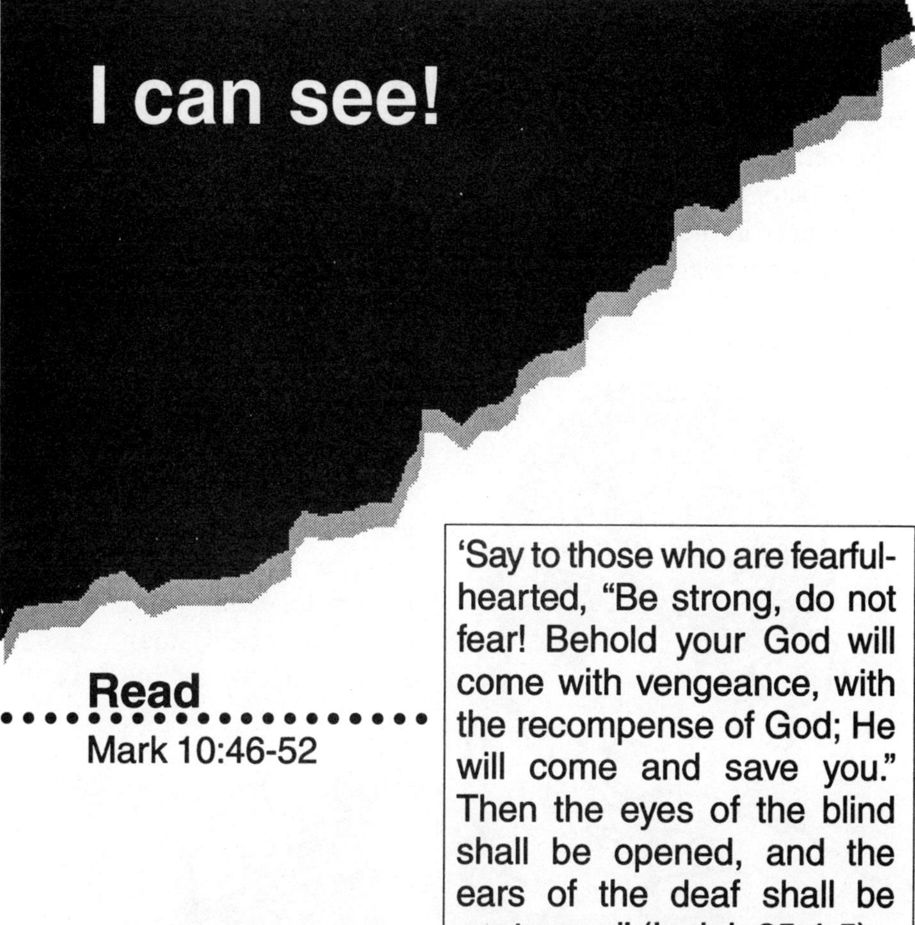

Read

Mark 10:46-52

> 'Say to those who are fearful-hearted, "Be strong, do not fear! Behold your God will come with vengeance, with the recompense of God; He will come and save you." Then the eyes of the blind shall be opened, and the ears of the deaf shall be unstopped' (Isaiah 35:4-5).

When I was a schoolteacher, I came into contact with many children who suffered from some kind of disability. One of the greatest challenges I had was when a young, almost blind, nine-year-old girl was enrolled at my school. This young person was totally blind in one eye and had only three per cent vision in the other. She had a lovely personality and was always trying to play games with the other children. Many times she ran into people and other objects, but even hurt and with tears in her eyes, she could still laugh. She did some of her lessons with the other children, but most of her lessons were with teachers who were specially trained to teach children with particular difficulties.

Blindness is an affliction and all who can see well should marvel at the way blind people cope with life. It is not until eyesight begins to fail that people really appreciate being able to see. We take so much for granted.

My daughter Heather wanted to be a doctor, but eventually studied to become an optician. When she started work one of the first requests she made of me was to get rid of my faithful glasses that I had used for many years. She said that the black frame was 'old-fashioned' and I needed to 'get with it'. So now I wear spectacles with what looks like a gold frame and multifocal lenses. I even have a spare pair to use when I can't find my good pair.

Sometimes we hear of a person who was blind regaining his or her sight. Today doctors can do great things with surgery. I know a doctor who was a missionary in India and was involved in eye clinics where blind people had their sight restored after surgery.

Our text reminds us that miracles were to bear testimony to the claims of Jesus that he was indeed the long-awaited Christ, the Son of God. We are told that the blind would see and the deaf would hear.

If you have read your Bible passage for today you will know about a blind man named Bartimaeus. To be blind in the days of the Lord Jesus was a tragedy. The government of the day didn't provide pensions for the blind. There were no eye hospitals. Most of the blind people would be forced to sit in the streets and beg for food or money from those who passed by. I can imagine plenty of beggars going without food on many occasions.

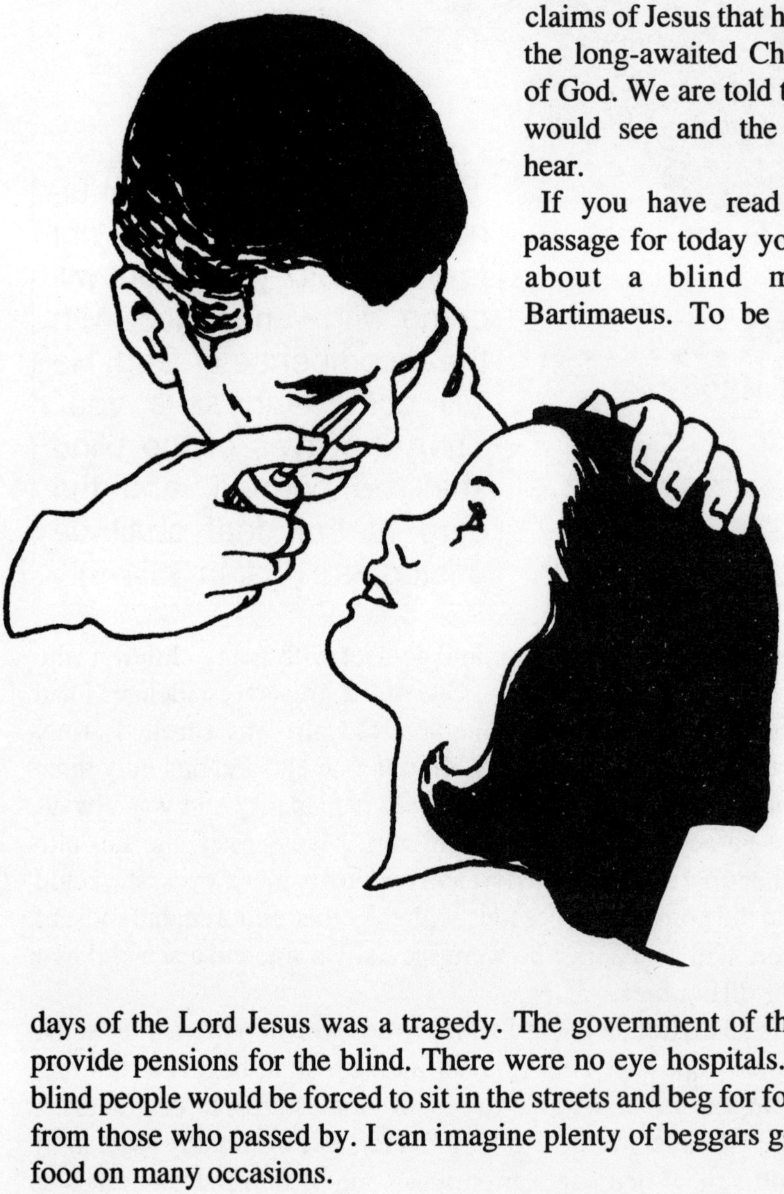

But Jesus was the one who healed the blind. I'm sure blind Bartimaeus had heard about Christ and the miracles he had performed. In fact we find him calling Jesus 'Son of David' (Mark 10:48). Can you try to imagine the excitement that must have filled his heart when he heard that Jesus was coming along the road where he sat begging? I'm sure Bartimaeus must have thought to himself, 'Here's my chance to get my sight. I've heard that Jesus has given blind people their sight. When he comes along the road, I'm going to get him to heal me!'

Bartimaeus no doubt heard the crowds speaking of Christ coming along the road, so he began to call out in his loudest voice, 'Jesus, Son of David, have mercy on me!' (v. 47). But the people standing near Bartimaeus didn't like him calling out loudly. Maybe they were embarrassed standing near a blind man who was shouting. So they told him to be quiet.

But Bartimaeus knew that Jesus was his only opportunity for healing. He probably thought, 'I must make Jesus hear me. This is my only chance to be healed.' He didn't care what people thought of him. He had to make Jesus hear him, so he called out even louder.

And then a wonderful thing happened. We read in verse 49 of our Bible reading for today, 'So Jesus stood still and commanded him to be called.'

There must have been a lot of noise that day, but Jesus heard Bartimaeus calling. He knew that there was a man who needed help. Jesus stopped still, probably listened again and then asked that the blind man be brought before him.

Jesus then asked Bartimaeus, 'What do you want Me to do for you?' Here was Bartimaeus' great opportunity. He told the Lord that he wanted his sight. The Lord immediately healed Bartimaeus.

Try to imagine the joy that filled the heart of this once blind man. He would have looked at Jesus. As he had been born blind, the face of Jesus must have been the first human face he had ever seen. How he loved the one who had given him his sight! We then read that he followed Jesus along the road.

I think that Bartimaeus would have become a sincere lover of Christ. One day, when we enter heaven, we shall meet this saint and no doubt hear him tell the story of how he gained his sight.

Reader, do you know that all humans are spiritually blind? Without the presence of God's Holy Spirit we cannot see Christ. The ordinary person has no real understanding of sin and the way of salvation. What sinners need is for the Holy Spirit to come into their souls and change their characters. Then they will be able to trust in Jesus.

But the Holy Spirit does not knock on the door of the heart every day. It could be that today the Spirit is convicting you of your sinfulness. It may be that even now you feel your need of a Saviour. The Spirit may not knock upon the door of your soul tomorrow. You need to be like blind Bartimaeus and cry out to Jesus: 'Lord, I need spiritual sight to understand my wickedness and my need of a Saviour. Lord, send the Holy Spirit into my life that I might be able to trust in Christ.'

Friends, do not put off turning to Jesus. Like Bartimaeus, it may be that Jesus passes by you just once. What a tragedy it would be if you ignored the Holy Spirit's call to repentance! If you are not a Christian may God lead you to Christ as you read the stories that follow.

Activities

1. Why was Jesus called 'Son of David'?
2. What makes us spiritually blind?
3. What is meant by 'The Holy Spirit is convicting you of your sins'?

STORY 32

Which fork do I use?

Read

Matthew 22:1-14

> 'Blessed are those who do His commandments, that they may have the right to the tree of life, and may enter through the gates into the city. But outside are dogs and sorcerers and sexually immoral and murderers and idolaters, and whoever loves and practises a lie' (Revelation 22:14-15).

It's not very pleasant to be somewhere you don't really want to be. My wife Valerie and I grew up on farms about forty kilometres from each other. I knew her brother as we went to high school together, but it was not till I went to teachers' college that I met Valerie. It was there we became sweethearts and some years later married.

But our life on the farm was a very simple one. Our parents worked hard each day and rarely were there holidays. As children we did our jobs about the farm and we lived too far from the town to go out very much. Even when we attended teachers' college, we didn't mix much with those people who were always out and about. I guess we have always tried to live a quiet and simple lifestyle.

Early in our married life we were posted to a small country school. Everyone in the area worked on farms and so we fitted in very well with the people. But as schoolteachers we found it necessary to mix with folk from the large city a few kilometres away. At that time I was teaching all day as well as completing my studies at the local university.

Not long after our arrival we received an invitation to a special dinner being given to new teachers in the area. When we arrived at the home we found about ten other teachers and their wives present. We talked about our schools, where we had come from, but both Valerie and I felt uneasy. The people present were very hospitable and did all they could to make us feel at home. Maybe we were young and inexperienced, but we felt a bit out of place.

Then came the time for our meal. We were escorted to a very large dining room, where there was a table large enough for all to sit around. The table was set in a beautiful way. Everything was just right. But when I sat

down I saw that there were two knives on one side of a plate and two forks on the other side. There were several spoons there as well. I looked at Valerie as I wasn't sure which knife and fork I was to use for the different courses. I hoped that she would whisper to me and tell me what to do.

The food came out and I couldn't begin to eat as I was afraid that I would do the wrong thing — I might use the wrong knife and fork. So I waited and watched. Then I did what others did. I eventually survived the night, but felt very much out of place. Valerie and I were happy to get back to the security of our home and our own way of life. (Although I now know my table etiquette, I still get worried if I find two or three forks beside my plate and usually wait for others to start eating, before I pick up my fork.) I'm sure there have been times when you too felt out of place. There must have been times when you wished you were somewhere else.

Our text and reading for today tell us the very same truth. As far as God is concerned there are two groups of people in the world — the saved and the unsaved. There is a great difference between these two groups of people. The saved — or the saints — are those who love God and serve Jesus Christ. They are people who love God's truth and practise righteousness. They are people who are born of God's Holy Spirit and are citizens of heaven. The unsaved are those who follow Satan. They are not interested in God's holiness. They have no true love for Jesus Christ as their Lord and Saviour.

The differences between the two groups of people are so great that they don't get on well together. The godless feel uncomfortable with the saints because they want to do what pleases them. Many of them swear, tell filthy jokes and mock Christ and his followers. They feel at home with like-minded people. The saints love the company (or should love the company) of other Christians. They have so much in common. They love the same God, are saved by the same Saviour, are born again of the same Holy Spirit and have the same destiny.

When the saints are placed in the company of the godless, they begin to feel uneasy. They are out of place. After all, the Bible tells us that we are 'strangers and pilgrims on the earth' (Hebrews 11:13). When godless people are placed in the company of a group of Christians they also feel uneasy. They too are out of place. They want to get back to their godless friends where they can feel at home.

In this world the two groups cannot avoid mixing with each other. There are a lot of uneasy feelings. But the day is coming when the two groups of people will be separated for ever. God's people will enter the new heavens and earth which have been prepared as a home for the saints. Around that heavenly home is a wall and the godless cannot enter.

But the godless would not want to enter heaven, for heaven is the land of holiness, which is hated by all unrepentant sinners. None of God's people will feel uncomfortable in heaven because they will be with like-minded people who love God and want to serve and praise Christ for ever.

Reader, how do you feel when you come into contact with Christians? Do you enjoy their company or have you the feeling that you want to get back with your godless friends?

The reading for today is about the man who was out of place at the wedding-feast. He was the only person dressed in his own clothes. The rest of the guests wore clothing given them by the king. The clothing that each of God's people must wear is not their own righteousness, which is as filthy rags, but the spotless righteousness of Jesus Christ. When we are made holy with the holiness of Christ, we shall be at home in heaven and never feel out of place.

Activities

1. What makes people feel out of place in some situations?
2. Why would godless people be unhappy in heaven?
3. Give five reasons why the saints will be happy in heaven.

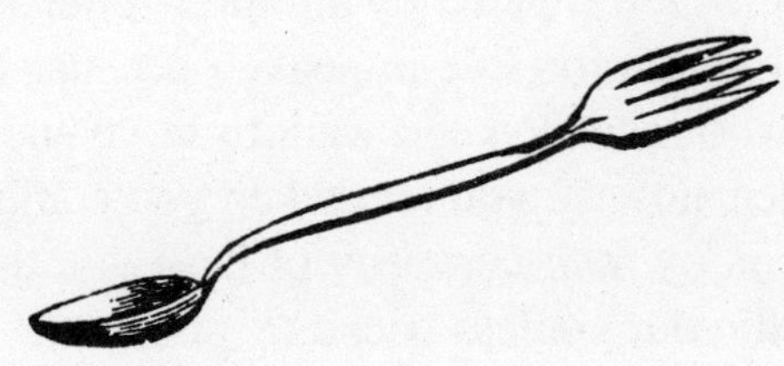

STORY 33

No one laughed!

Read
1 Corinthians 12:12-27

'For in fact the body is not one member but many... And if one member suffers, all the members suffer with it; or if one member is honoured, all the members rejoice with it' (1 Corinthians 12:14,26).

When I meet with other Christians, whether they are members of my congregation or some other congregation, I always regard these people as my brothers and sisters in Christ. We are all united in our worship of King Jesus, our Lord and Saviour. And the apostle Paul tells us that the church is really made up of all the saints of all ages.

Our reading for today tells you that the church is a body of believers, each one being different to one another. When you go to worship I'm sure you see young people, old people, men and women, rich people and poor people, some very well dressed and some in clothes that have been worn many times. Everyone is different.

Christians have to learn to live with each other. In a family brothers and sisters have squabbles, I'm sure, but you learn to live with each other. You learn to overlook the faults of your brothers and sisters. You learn to forgive any member of your family who hurts you. You even learn to laugh with your family members, and sometimes you will cry when they cry. This must be the same in the church. What affects one Christian should have an effect upon all Christians who know that person. The church, Paul tells us, is like a human body — many parts — and what happens to one part has an effect upon another part.

Many years ago, when I was fifteen years of age, I was able to get a job during school holidays at a factory that made masonite. This factory was about fifteen kilometres from our home on the farm, and I had to ride my bike to and from the factory every day. I worked mostly day shifts, but there were times when I started work in the middle of the night. However, they paid good money and I was very pleased to earn my own pocket money. Times were hard on the farm.

My first job was working in the stores, where there was everything that was needed to keep the factory running. If something broke down, the stores department would get the part and send it up to the workers who would get the machinery going again. This job was very easy and I enjoyed it very much. But the workmen were always playing jokes on me. I remember the day one fellow came and asked for a tin of striped paint. I started to look, and then realized what a fool I was.

As I grew older I was moved to a different section of the factory. One job I was given I didn't like at all. Sheets of masonite came down a shute and with another man I grabbed a sheet and put it in a pile. I did that for eight hours each day — the same thing over and over again. I was so bored I asked if there was another job I could do. The foreman was very kind and said I could move to the section where crates were made to hold twelve sheets of masonite. I was given a hammer and a bag of nails and sent to a steel table where there were three other men. Each of us worked at the corner of the table. We would each pick up a piece of timber and lay the planks to form a rectangle. Then we would hammer a triangular piece of tin to the planks so that a firm rectangle would be made. This was the first step in making the masonite crate.

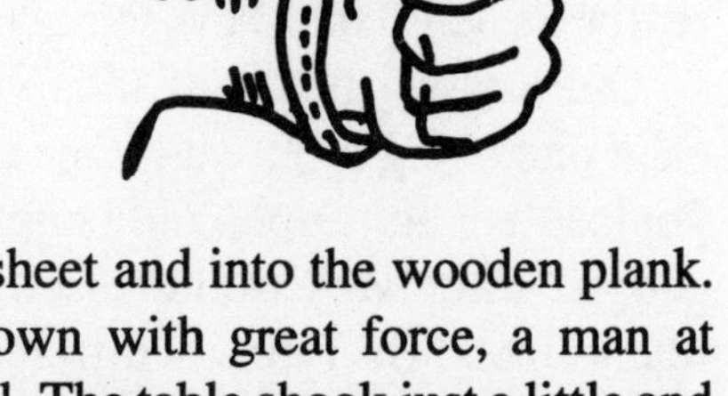

It looked easy work, but I soon found out that it was very dangerous. I held my nail carefully between my fingers, ready to drive it through the tin sheet and into the wooden plank. But just as my hammer was coming down with great force, a man at another corner of the steel table hit his nail. The table shook just a little and I missed the nail I was holding and the hammer hit my thumb!

Blood squirted out of my finger and within seconds my whole thumb was black and blue. A pain shot up my arm and I groaned and put my thumb in my mouth. No one laughed at me and then I saw why. Every man had sticking-plasters on his fingers. In days past they too had hit their

fingers with their hammers. They knew how I felt. One came over to me and said I should see the factory nurse. By the time I reached the sick bay, my head was aching, my whole hand was throbbing, blood was on my clothes and the whole of my body felt terrible.

Soon I was bandaged up and sent back to work. For the rest of that shift I was very careful and I didn't hit my thumb again that day. When I arrived home from work, Mum and Dad fussed over me. My thumb was still aching the next day when I went back to work. But I was super careful after that as I worked.

However, about a month later it happened again. Only this time, not only was there blood squirting everywhere and a blackened, swollen finger, but I could see the bone poking through the flesh. My whole body ached, even though just a finger was hurt. I had a few days off work, and when I returned was sent back to the stores department.

What happened to my body when I hit my thumb with the hammer is what should happen in the church when one member has a difficult time. No one should laugh, but everyone should help that person. No one should say, 'It served him right.' There are times when we should weep with someone who is weeping. Of course there are times when something wonderful happens to a church member. We should not be jealous of that person's success, but rejoice with him or her.

Christian friends, we all need to have a right attitude to our brothers and sisters in Christ. We shall live with them for ever. On earth we must love one another and that means we tolerate each other — even those who are difficult. We are all different, we all do different works, but we all love Jesus Christ and are loved by him. We must all learn to get on well with one another. We must all learn to love one another with Christian love.

Activities

1. Why can a Christian call another Christian 'a brother or sister in Christ'?
2. Why should a Christian rejoice with another Christian who is rejoicing?
3. What should a Christian do when another Christian is in trouble?
4. What is meant by 'Christian love'?

STORY 34

A very fortunate boy

Read

John 1:1-13

'"I will be a Father to you, and you shall be My sons and daughters," says the LORD Almighty' (2 Corinthians 6:18).

Most of my readers, if not all, belong to a family. Some will have a mum and dad and maybe brothers and sisters. Others may live with mum or dad and some will live with grandparents or relatives or friends. However, there are children who for some reason or other live in orphanages, or children's homes, with other children. There are also quite a few people who are adopted and live with new parents who take care of them.

I remember I once taught a boy who was adopted. He was a lovely young fellow and all he wanted to do with his life was to become a carpenter and work in his father's business. He was very intelligent and I thought that he was more suited to other work. But he said, 'Dad makes a lot of money building houses, so I am going to become a carpenter and work for him. When I get older I will be able to take over his business.'

He was about twelve years of age and one day came to school and told me that his mother and father had told him the night before that he was their adopted son. I asked him how he felt about learning that he was adopted.

He said to me, 'I love my mum and dad. And there is a special reason I love them — they picked me out to be their son.' He didn't seem to be too concerned that he was adopted, and was never afraid to tell his friends of the fact.

Later that week I met his parents and they asked me how Bill was getting on at school. He was a good student and a very pleasant boy. It was obvious they loved him very much. I told them that Bill had spoken to me and his friends about the fact that he was adopted. I asked them why they had told him about his adoption.

The parents said that they wanted Bill to hear this from them and not find out some other way. Then I was told that Bill had been born to an unmarried mother who could not look after him. She had thought it best if her son was adopted as she had very little to offer him. So it was that Bill found his way into a family that took him as their son and loved him very much. The other children in the family were told of Bill's adoption at the same time as their mum and dad broke the news to Bill.

Everyone in that family loved one another and the fact that Bill had been adopted didn't cause any problems. In fact I think Bill loved his adopted parents even more after he had the facts revealed to him.

Bill was really a wonderful member of his adopted family. I guess he had many more privileges in that family than he could have had if he had grown up with his true mum. Some years later Bill found his mum and they became good friends, but he always looked upon his adopted parents as his real mum and dad.

Bill left primary school, attended secondary school, and became a carpenter. I always thought he could have used his intelligence in some other way, but his dad made him a partner in the building firm and it wasn't long before Bill had a car and a plot of land. In his spare time he was going to build a home.

I don't know what has happened to Bill, but he was a very sensible young man, had a great occupation and seemed very happy knowing that he was adopted. Bill's adoption did great things for him. I imagine that with the other children in the family he would have inherited the family business.

We all belonged to the family of Satan until God changed our hearts making it possible for us to repent of our sins and trust in Jesus Christ as Lord and Saviour. Then, as the Bible tells us, we were taken from the family of Satan and adopted into God's family. When this happens God is no longer to be feared, and we can call him, 'Abba, Father' (Romans 8:15). The word 'Abba' was a lovely word used by children in Israel as a special name for their father. We might say it is like 'Dad' or 'Dearest Dad'.

Those whom God saves are adopted into God's family and we become his sons and daughters. Then Paul tells us that we become 'joint heirs with Christ' (Romans 8:17). This means that all the spiritual treasures that belong to Christ are ours as well. We have a home in heaven. We shall inherit the new earth. We shall see Christ face to face. God will wipe away our tears and we shall enjoy him for ever.

Reader, are you a member of God's family? Have you been adopted so that you are now a brother or sister of Jesus Christ? If not, you must ask God to send his Spirit into your heart that you might believe in Jesus. Then, and then only, will you be an adopted son or daughter of the living God.

Activities

1. What is meant by 'adoption'?
2. Who can call God 'Abba, Father' ? What does this expression mean?
3. Who is the Christian's 'elder brother'?
4. Jesus was God's Son. In what way are Christians sons and daughters of God?

STORY 35

A friend for life

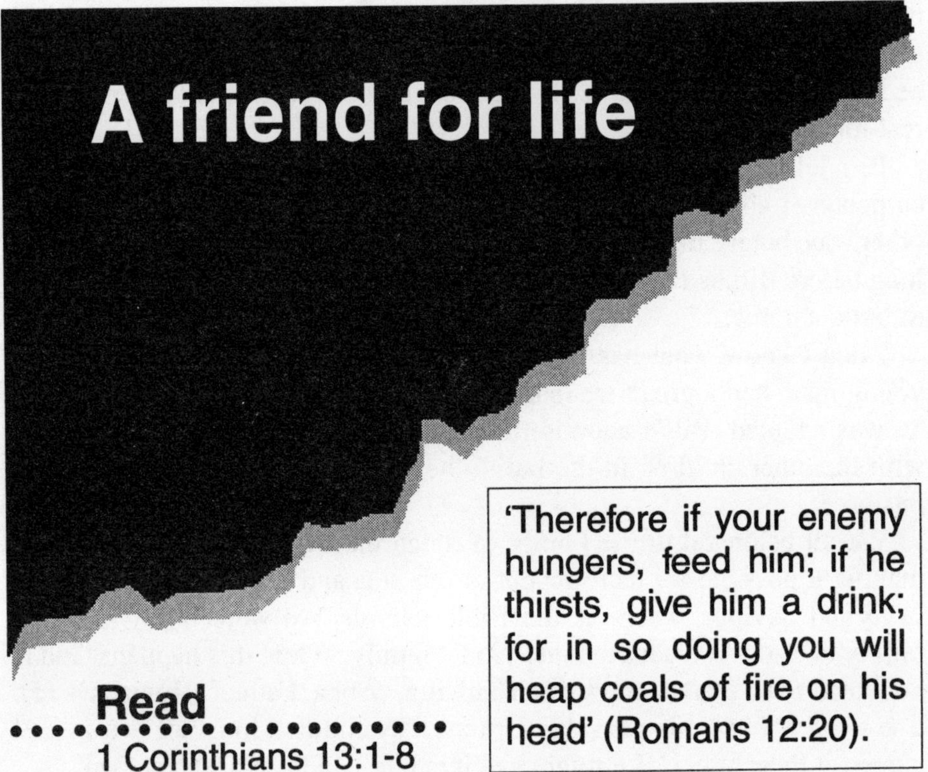

Read

1 Corinthians 13:1-8

'Therefore if your enemy hungers, feed him; if he thirsts, give him a drink; for in so doing you will heap coals of fire on his head' (Romans 12:20).

Our text for today is a strange one. I feel sure that if we put coals of fire on a person's head we should not be very popular. How is it possible that by feeding someone who hates me, or giving a drink to a thirsty enemy, I heap coals of fire on his head?

God demands of his people that we love others. This doesn't mean that we must be willing to give everyone a hug and a kiss, but it does mean that we must always do things that will not harm anyone — things that are for their good. When you read the Bible passage for today you will learn what Christian love is like.

It is good for you to be friends with everyone at school. But this is not always possible. I remember that when I was at primary school there was one boy who always picked on me. He was bigger than I was and I was afraid of him. Eight of us used to leave school each day at the same time. We each had bikes and lived about five kilometres from the school. It was Tom who seemed to tell everyone what to do. If anyone didn't do as he said, he would give that person a good punch. So everyone did as he said.

Tom was a bully. The rest of us didn't like him, but were too frightened to stand up to him. Tom could make life very miserable and there were

days when I didn't want to go to school, because Tom had told me he would 'get me' the next morning.

One day as we were riding home from school, Tom had a fall from his bike. There was a hole in the road and the wheel on his bike had twisted when it hit the hole. He fell very heavily to the road. When we all stopped we could see tears in his eyes. He had lumps of skin missing from his arms and legs and there was a lot of blood about. We could all see that he was hurt and needed help.

I imagine that the other boys felt the same way as I did. I can still remember thinking, 'It serves him right. He deserves to be hurt.' We all rode our bikes back to Tom. He didn't ask for our help. Maybe he thought that no one would help him because he had treated us so badly. However, we all helped him to his feet and used our handkerchiefs to mop up the blood. We fussed over Tom. Maybe we were too frightened to do anything else. Eventually we got him back to his home. His mother thanked us for helping him and Tom even said, 'Thanks'.

For several days Tom was missing from school. He had really hurt himself. And when he returned to school, Tom treated us as his friends. He didn't bully us any more. In fact Tom went out of his way to help us and we all became good friends. We can sometimes make a friend out of an enemy by doing a good turn. How can this be called heaping 'coals of fire on his head'?

Imagine that you lived in the days of the apostle Paul. How would you light a fire? There were no matches or cigarette lighters in those days. The Australian aborigines rubbed two sticks together to make a fire. In other parts of the world hard stones were struck together to get a spark.

In the days when our text was written if a home had a fire going it would have been unwise to let it go out, because it was such a problem to get it started again.

Let's imagine that the man living next door didn't like your family. He let his dog into your garden and was always arguing with your mum and dad. But one night he forgot to stoke the fire and in the morning, when his wife was ready to cook breakfast there were no hot coals in the hearth. Maybe the man was in a hurry and didn't have time to get a decent fire going, so he decided to come to your home and ask for a red hot coal to take home to start his fire.

When he knocked on your door, he had a large jug that he carried on his head. He said, 'I'm sorry to trouble you, but could you please give me a little hot coal to get my fire going again?' Maybe Mum and Dad would think, 'Serves him right.' But Mum and Dad are Christians and they want to show Christian love by helping this man who was a pest to them. To show that love they don't give him the smallest red coal, but put a shovel full of red hot coals in his earthenware jar. The man, when he has thanked your mum and dad for their kindness, puts the jug on his head and walks back home. You have heaped coals of fire on his head in an act of kindness. When he gets home and tells his wife of the kindness of your family, he decides to be a friend and show kindness instead of anger.

God showed his great love to sinners who hated him. He was willing to send his Son, Jesus Christ, into the world to bear the sins of his people. When you understand what Jesus has done for you, he will be your Friend and you will love and serve him for ever.

My Christian reader, are you doing all you can to make friends of those who treat you badly? By God's grace you can do so.

Activities

1. Look at the text for today. What does it mean?
2. How can you make a friend of a person who does not like you? What do you do if your attempts to win the person's friendship do not work?
3. How did God show his love for sinners? Find John 3:16 in your Bible. Learn that text (if you haven't already done so) and discuss what it means.

Look out, bald eagle!

Read

2 Kings 2

'Honour all people. Love the brotherhood. Fear God. Honour the king' (1 Peter 2:17).

'You shall rise before the grey-headed and honour the presence of an old man, and fear your God: I am the LORD' (Leviticus 19:32).

Last Sunday as I was getting ready for worship, I stood in front of the mirror to comb my hair. I noticed that the light was shining brightly on the skin that was poking through my hair. Running the comb through the few remaining hairs I suddenly thought — another few years and there would be no hair left on my head. I wouldn't have to worry about combs, as I would have no hair to comb. I wouldn't have to go to the hairdresser any more and I would save the money I usually spent getting haircuts.

During worship I looked about and noticed a few other men of my age who also had the same problem. Then I looked at the pastor in the pulpit. Pastor Peter had a lovely, well-kept beard, but the light was shining brightly on his balding head.

The principal of one school at which I taught was bald — or almost bald. He had a ring of white hair around a large bald patch on top of his head. He was a very nice fellow and was popular with the children.

One day when he arrived at school, he was not in a very good mood. I asked him, 'What's wrong, John?'

'Well,' he replied, 'as I was walking to school someone yelled out, "Bald eagle!" When I turned around there was no one in sight. I started walking again and then there came the same yell — "Bald eagle!" Someone must have been hiding. I don't know who it was, but if I find out there'll be trouble.'

In those days I had plenty of hair and just smiled at poor John. But whoever yelled out at the school principal in that cheeky way was showing no respect for a man who had done a lot of good for many children and adults in the town.

Our text for today reminds us that we are to honour all people. This means that we respect our parents and all the people we meet day by day, especially those in authority. We are not to be rude to others, but show true Christian love. We are to speak words of kindness to others and always do those things which are pleasing to both God and man. If people acted in this way the world would be a much happier place. God commands us to show honour to the aged. In our text we are reminded that we should rise before the older person. In this way we show our love and respect for that person. Too often people treat the aged as useless people not worth worrying about.

When I was young and grew up on a farm, my grandparents lived and worked on the farm too. My brother and I loved our aged grandparents and we wept many tears when they died. They died, not in hospital, but at home. I well remember my grandfather calling each family member to his bedside one by one to say farewell just before he died. I was about ten years old and can clearly remember his words telling me that he was going to be with Christ and then urging me to trust in and serve Jesus as my Lord and Saviour.

We have much to learn from the elderly and it would do us all good to sit and listen to the wisdom of many of the elderly saints. Show the aged that you love and respect them.

In our reading for today we find one of God's greatest prophets, Elisha, being mocked by some young men — probably teenagers. These teenagers had heard about Elijah being taken up to heaven without passing through death. When Elisha appeared in their town these young men went out and began to laugh at him. He also was bald on top, but he was a great man of God. Those young men should have shown him honour, but they called out, 'Go up, you bald head!' What they meant was, 'Elisha, you old bald-headed person, you go up to heaven as did Elijah!' In anger, God sent two bears who mauled the forty-two youths.

Reader, do you understand that we are to respect the government of the day? We are to remember that our parliamentarians are placed there by God for our good. We are to honour the king or queen, or the prime minister, or the president of our country. We are to pray for those who rule over us.

We are also to show honour to God in everything we do. Do you honour your minister and church elders? Do you honour your Sunday School teachers? Do you respect the aged? I pray so, because if you do, you are being obedient to God's commands.

Activities

1. What did the young men mean when they said to Elisha, 'Go up, you bald head!'?
2. Who was Elisha?
3. Why should you respect and pray for those who rule us?

STORY 37

God is no man's debtor

Read

2 Corinthians 9:1-14

'"Bring all the tithes into the storehouse, that there may be food in My house, and prove Me now in this," says the LORD of Hosts, "if I will not open for you the windows of heaven and pour out for you such blessing that there will not be room enough to receive it"' (Malachi 3:10).

It is very true that God is no man's debtor. We owe God everything and he owes us nothing. As sinners we have no claim on God's goodness whatsoever. All the blessings which we receive from God's hand are due to the saving work of the Lord Jesus Christ, who paid the penalty due to his people for sin and lived the life of holiness in their place. Jesus has won for us blessings beyond anything we can ever imagine.

The greatest blessing he has won for us is the love of God which floods our heart, if we are Christians. And while God owes us nothing but his anger because of our sins, he is very gracious and gives so much to all. The sun shines on the Christian and the godless alike. The rain falls on all people, not just the saints.

In Old Testament days, the saints were found mostly in the land of Israel, for this was the land which was given to God's people as their own special land. God demanded of his people that they be holy. The Jewish people were to love God and to serve him faithfully. When they did this they were just doing what they should have been doing. God owed them nothing, but when he saw their faithfulness in service and worship he blessed them greatly. The rain would come at the proper time and the crops would grow. There would be peace in the nation. God does not have to reward faithfulness, yet he does. God is no man's debtor.

In our text we find God challenging the Jewish people to test him. The Jews were unfaithful to God at this time in their history. They were not serving God as required and as a result God withheld the rain and their barns were soon emptied of food. So we read God's challenge, spoken through the prophet Malachi: 'Test Me! Be faithful to Me — bring in your tithes to the temple and wait and watch. I will bless the land with rain and you will have so much food that the barns and sheds you have will not be big enough to hold it all.'

Our God has not changed. He is the same God today as he was in the days of Malachi. He always keeps his promises.

Today the saints do not have an earthly country to call their own. God's people are spread throughout the world. God's blessings are first of all spiritual, but he also blesses many of his faithful people with great material blessings. God is no man's debtor.

Some years ago I was the congregational treasurer. It was my job to collect all the offerings made on the Lord's Day, count the money and make sure it was banked. I had to enter in a book all the givings and the expenses. At the end of each year the books were audited to make sure no money was missing.

One day after counting the collection for the Lord's Day, I carefully hid the money on top of the wardrobe, as I knew that neither my wife nor I could do the banking on Monday. After school on Monday, we returned home and walked in the back door. It was locked as it should have been. My habit was then to walk through the house, out the front door and collect the mail.

When I came to the front door I found it unlocked. That didn't concern me as we lived in a quiet street and many times we left the door unlocked. After all, my wife had only been away from the house for half an hour or so. She had come down to the school to collect me and the children. But as I walked through the front door I noticed that the fly screen was on the verandah. Even that didn't bother me as I knew the wind could sometimes blow fly screens off. But suddenly I had a horrible thought: 'Has someone broken into the house?'

'Val,' I called, with a sinking feeling in my heart, 'I think someone's been in the house while you were away. Is the church money still on top of the cupboard?'

But sure enough all the money was missing. The cheques were still there, but the coins and notes were gone. Also there were clothes strewn about in the bedroom. The children ran into their rooms and they, too, discovered that some of their treasures were missing.

We rang the police, but they said that finding the thief would be like looking for a needle in a haystack. Many months later the thief was caught, because she came back another day and stole some more things.

However, the church offering was missing and I felt responsible for the loss. So Valerie and I decided to take the money out of our bank account and replace what had been stolen. But I was soon to learn that God was no man's debtor.

About a fortnight after I had replaced about one thousand dollars, I found what turned out to be a special letter in the letter-box. It was addressed to me and when I opened the envelope I found a cheque for one thousand dollars. That night I rang my brother John to tell him what had happened. He was rejoicing as he too had received a cheque in the mail — also for one thousand dollars. A dear aunt, who looked upon John and me as the sons she never had, decided to send us each a gift. She had not known about the theft of the church money.

I could hardly believe my eyes when I saw the cheque. God had replaced our money so simply and easily. God is no man's debtor.

Sometimes we shall not see the blessing that God has for us till we reach heaven. But God will always fulfil his promises, because he loves his dear Son Jesus Christ who saved all who trust in him.

In the reading for today we read of Paul asking the churches to give to those congregations in need. Paul tells us that God loves a cheerful giver. He also tells us that if we give just the leftovers God will not bless us as greatly as when we give much and rejoice in doing so. God does not ask us to give away everything we have so that others might have plenty and we have nothing. But Christians are expected to help those in need — especially other Christians.

Christian friend, are you a joyful giver to those who are in need? I trust so. Always remember what God gave to you. God gave us his Son Jesus Christ to die upon a cross that we might be saved. We owe God everything.

Activities

1. Read the text for today. What was God telling the Jewish people?
2. What is meant by the words: 'God is no man's debtor'?
3. Does God owe humans anything at all?
4. What do Christians owe to God?

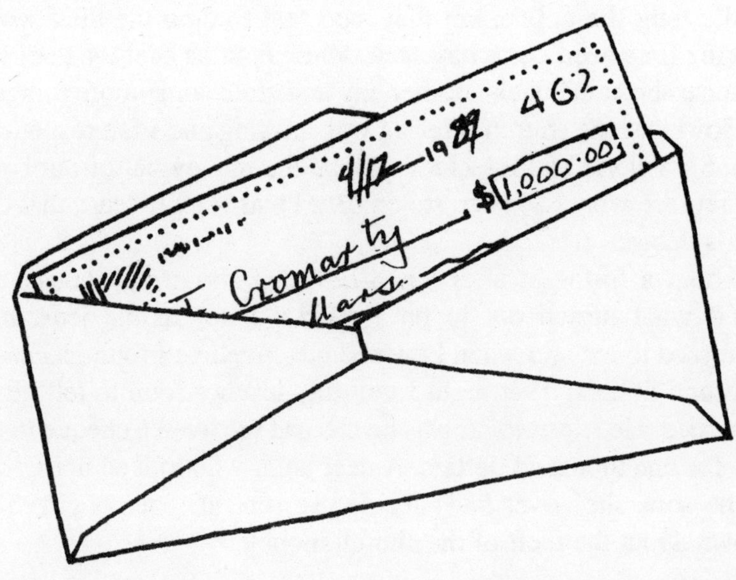

STORY 38

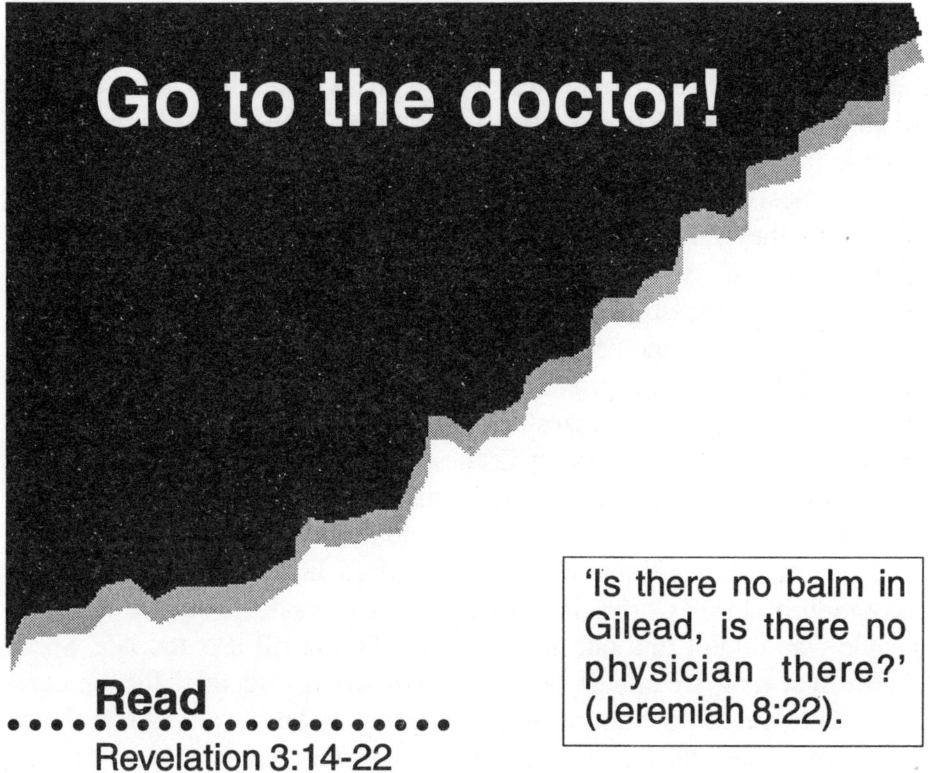

Go to the doctor!

Read

Revelation 3:14-22

> 'Is there no balm in Gilead, is there no physician there?' (Jeremiah 8:22).

I don't like visiting the doctor. When I get sick I usually go to the chemist and get some over-the-counter medicine and trust that I will recover. My wife is a lot more sensible about these things. Her advice is, 'Go to the doctor and get the correct treatment. You'll recover in half the time.' But like most men I keep away from the doctor as much as I can.

Now refusing to go to the doctor is silly and can be very dangerous. In fact I know a man who lost his life because he delayed going to the doctor. The man was dying of cancer. The cancer had moved into his bones and he was very ill. I went to visit this stranger and did so over the last two years of his life. In fact I was with him when he died. I had just read the Scriptures to him and prayed, when he stopped breathing. He knew something was wrong with his health, but he left it too long to visit the doctor. By the time he had surgery the cancer had spread throughout his

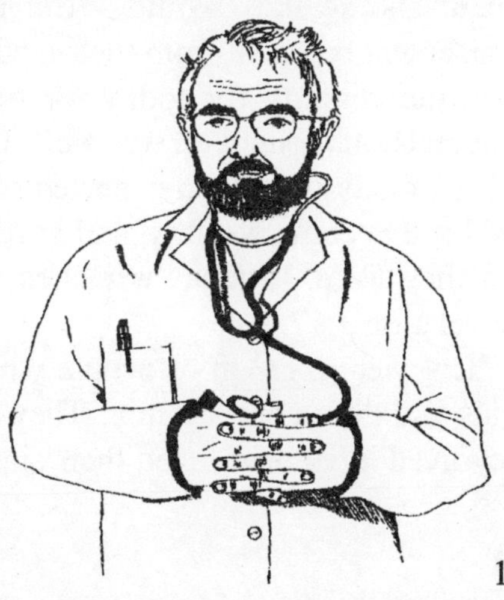

body and was in his bones. If he had gone to the doctor earlier, the result may have been different.

There are many people who know they are not well physically — they feel ill, yet refuse to go to the doctor for a check-up. Others know they are ill and head off to the doctor after a long time. Then the doctor makes an error in his diagnosis and the person gets much worse. In some cases they die. But most doctors know what they are doing. They carry out tests, keep testing till they find out what is wrong and then they are able to give the correct treatment. We should thank God that he has given us men and women to look after our health.

Then there are some people who are very ill and do not realize till it is too late. Some sicknesses just eat away at our bodies and have few symptoms. By the time the person realizes that something is really wrong, the doctor finds it almost impossible to repair the damage. There are some even who think they are in perfect health and all the time are desperately ill.

Now, readers, whether you know it or not, you all have a disease — and that disease is called sin! Every person born into this world, with the exception of Jesus Christ, is born with this disease. There are so many people who do not find out they have the disease till it is too late. Some realize that they are sinners and go to the wrong 'doctors' for the cure. Then there are those who know they are sinners because God has shown this to them, and they go to the only Doctor who can heal them of their disease — the Lord Jesus Christ.

Our text refers to the Jews who had rebelled against God and were about to be severely punished. Jeremiah the prophet is really calling them to repent of their sins. If they did this then God would forgive them and save them from the invading army.

Gilead was a town in Judah, well known for making an ointment which helped wounds to heal. If a person needed a doctor to treat a wound, the best doctors and the best ointment were at Gilead. And there was a great Doctor in Judah who could heal sin — the Lord. But the people would not repent and so they would suffer invasion by the Babylonians and as punishment be taken from their land for seventy years.

In our reading for today we read of the church at Laodicea. This congregation thought all was well. The members thought their church was doing exactly what God expected of them. Their attitude was: 'I am rich, and have become wealthy, and have need of nothing.' They did not know that they were, in fact, 'wretched, miserable, poor, blind, and naked...' (Revelation 3:17).

Here were a group of people who thought that all was well with their souls and their congregation. They thought they were loved by God, yet they lived in sin and loved their sins. Jesus urged them to see the Doctor who could heal them of their spiritual sickness. Like Jeremiah who preached to the Jews of old and called them to repentance, so Jesus called the Laodiceans to repentance.

They needed Jesus in order to have their eyes opened to see their sins. They needed the perfect righteousness of Jesus to cover their sins. They had pushed Jesus out of their church. Now they had to repent if they were to be saved. Healing was there, if only they realized that they needed healing. That congregation did not repent of their sins and eventually ceased to exist.

Friend, do you truly understand that you are a sinner and under God's condemnation? If you say to yourself, 'Well, I may do some things that are not right, but I'm not as bad as others; I do many good things, so God must love me,' then you are fooling yourself. You can't heal the disease of sin. Only Jesus can do that — so to Jesus you must go. You must confess your sin and then seek that healing which comes from him alone. His righteousness is the ointment you need to cover your sins. His death upon the cross is needed by you to pay the penalty for your sins.

Reader, if you are not a Christian, then whether you like it or not, you are spiritually sick and dying. In fact you are spiritually dead. Only Jesus can heal you and make you live. Go to him in true repentance and seek life. Read your Bible and ask God to open your spiritual eyes so that you might see the truth that is contained within its pages.

Activities

1. From what disease do all humans suffer?
2. What is the remedy for this disease?
3. What is sin?
4. Why is sin so terrible?

STORY 39

A change of heart

'Can the Ethiopian change his skin or the leopard its spots? Then may you also do good who are accustomed to do evil' (Jeremiah 13:23).

Read

John 3:1-8

I have seen leopards at the zoo and they are spotty creatures. Our text speaks of the leopard and asks the question: 'Is it possible for a leopard to somehow change its colouring by getting rid of its spots?' Of course the answer is, 'No!' A leopard has spots and that's that. By itself it cannot get rid of its spots.

We are like the leopard in some ways. We are born into this world as sinners and there is not a thing we can do by ourselves to get rid of the stain of sin. We can't wish our sins away. We are sinners. That's that, and by ourselves we cannot change our sinful nature any more than the leopard can get rid of its spots.

But the wonderful thing is that God can get rid of the stain of sin found in our being. God can change our sinful nature and make us new people in Christ Jesus the Saviour. What you and I can't do, God can do.

Have you ever tried to change the colour of a white flower? You're not allowed to spray-paint the flower — anyone can do that! Are you able to make a white flower into a red flower by changing its colour inside? The answer is 'Yes'. Simply put the stem of a white flower into some red ink or colouring and before long you will see the flower changing colour. The white petals will gradually become pink as the red liquid is sucked up the flower's stem. The change is remarkable and it takes place inside the flower, but can be seen on the outside.

God does change sinners and make them new creatures who hate sin. This is known as being 'born again'. The change takes place when the Holy Spirit enters the heart and gives the gift of faith to the sinner. The Holy Spirit also makes it possible for the sinner to repent of his or her sins, and the blood of Christ which was shed upon the cross at Calvary is able to cleanse from sin. The holiness of Christ is given to his people and so all Christians are new creatures.

Our reading for today tells us of Nicodemus who went to Jesus at night-time to find out all he could about this great miracle-worker and teacher. Nicodemus was told that he needed to be born again — to be born 'of God' (John 1:13).

Just as the white flower changes its colour when the red ink is sucked up the stem, so also you will know when you are 'born again'. You will hate sin and love holiness. You will love God and the people about you. You will want to attend worship and mix with other Christians.

Reader, are you 'born again'? Have you repented of your sins? If you would enter heaven, you must be born again by God's Holy Spirit.

Activities

1. What do the Dalmatian dog and the leopard have in common?
2. Can a leopard get rid of its spots?
3. How can sinners get rid of the stain of sin?
4. What is meant by repentance?

STORY 40

God's eye is watching

Read

Psalm 139:7-12

'O God, You know my foolishness; and my sins are not hidden from You' (Psalm 69:5).

There are many times when we do something and think that no one is watching, but later someone tells us what we did. It is very difficult to do something in secret. When I was young we always had a big water-melon patch on the farm. During the summer months there would always be water melons to eat. We planted the seeds every couple of weeks so we had a continual supply during the hot summer months. Almost every afternoon, when the heat of the day was still strong, we took the water melon out of the tub of water under the house and then dropped it onto the ground. The ripe melon would break open and we would see the red flesh ready to be eaten. Mum or Dad would then cut up the melon and there we would sit, chomping into the melon, with the juice running down our cheeks.

One morning we noticed a car pull up down the road beside the water-melon patch, which was about a kilometre from our home. A man stepped out and we watched him looking about to see if anyone was in sight. He thought he was all alone — that no one was watching as he stole the water melons. Then he climbed under the fence, took some of the water melons and put them in the boot of his car. But Mum was outside and had seen what had taken place. As the car came along the road towards our home she

walked to the side of the road and waved her arms for the man to stop. Instead of stopping, he put his foot down on the accelerator and roared off past Mum. He must have known that he had been seen stealing the water melons.

Several kilometres down the road there was a small ferry to take the traffic across the river and we knew the man would have to stop his car when he reached that spot. Mum then rang a farmer who lived beside the road near the ferry and told him what had happened.

When the farmer friend confronted the man who had stolen the water melons, the thief denied that he had stolen anything. He even opened the boot of his car to show that there were no water melons there. Later that day Dad drove our car slowly down the road to the ferry and my brother John and I had the job of looking out of the car window to see if we could find any water melons on the roadside. We did! That man was a thief, who thought no one could see what he was doing. But he was seen.

Our text tells us that God knows all that we do. We cannot escape from his presence. That's why the psalmist asks the question: 'Where can I go from Your Spirit? Or where can I flee from Your presence?' (Psalm 139:7). The psalmist then answers his questions by telling us that God is everywhere. Our sins are not hidden from him. If we were always to remember that the eye of God is upon us, surely we would be more careful of obeying God's law. However, always remember that the reason why Christians obey the law of God is because we love God and his Son, Jesus Christ.

In Luke 8:43-48 we read of a sick woman who simply touched the clothing of Jesus and was healed. She thought that Jesus had not noticed what she did. But Jesus knew what had happened. He knew what that woman had done. Nothing can be hidden from Christ.

Reader, think of the coming Judgement Day. How will things be for you on that day? Remember, the eye of God is upon you at all times. He knows everything you have done. Nothing has been hidden from God. Will your sins drag you to hell, or have they been forgiven and forgotten by God, because you trust in the Lord Jesus Christ alone for your salvation?

May God be pleased to show each of you your sin. And may God show you the way of salvation which is found in Christ the Saviour.

Activities

1. How is it that God can see everything you do?
2. Why should Christians obey the road rules?
3. Do you obey your parents all the time or just when they are watching you? Why did you give that answer?

STORY 41

I'll wash you!

Read

Philippians 3:1-9

'Therefore we conclude that a man is justified by faith apart from the deeds of the law' (Romans 3:28).

The apostle Paul was in his younger days a great Pharisee, and he was immensely proud of it. In our reading for today we read of the things that once mattered to Paul. He was an Israelite, one of God's chosen people. He was a Pharisee, one of the religious leaders who thought that God loved them in a special way because they obeyed his law. But Paul had to learn an important fact — all of his good works, his obedience to God's law, could not save him. He had to depend upon the work of the Lord Jesus Christ for his salvation. Now it is hard to depend upon others, especially when you have been able to do things for yourself.

Some time ago I was forced to enter hospital for back surgery. Before I went to hospital doctors had treated me, but I wasn't the best of patients and continued to get about as best I could carrying out my duties as a pastor of a congregation. I found it very difficult to drive the car, and my wife Valerie became my taxi driver. Also, Stewart, a member of the congregation, used to drive me every month to one of my congregations about one hundred kilometres away.

I had to depend upon others, and didn't find it too difficult to accept the help offered. I found difficulty in standing and used to preach sitting down.

But eventually the doctors said I needed surgery and so it wasn't long before I found myself in an operating theatre ready to be put to sleep. Before I fell asleep I could see scalpels, probes, needles and thread and other terrible-looking instruments just waiting to be used on me.

Following the surgery I was eventually returned to my bed. My back was aching and there were tubes hanging out of me here and there. I couldn't move and when I asked for a drink of water a nurse came and said, 'Now don't you move. I'll put a drinking straw into the glass and you can drink that way.' I suddenly found out that I was dependent upon the nurses for everything. But worse was to come.

Later that day a nurse appeared with a bowl of warm water. I thought that surely I could wash myself. No one had washed me since I was a very young person. But the nurse said, 'Now, you just lie quietly while I wash you.'

She unbuttoned my pyjama coat and sponged my upper body. It was really refreshing and made me forget about my aches and pains for a couple of minutes. But then the nurse, a young woman, said, 'Right, down with your pyjama trouser. Don't move. I'll get them down easily.' All I could say was, 'Just a minute, I can wash myself!' But as I tried to move I found that I couldn't. I was drugged to help control the pain and every movement caused a lot of pain. I was completely at the mercy of the young nurse, who washed me almost all over. Several days later I was allowed to have a shower, and the same nurse helped me to the bathroom. She told me she was there to help me have my shower. I tried to tell her I would cope by myself, but I soon found out I couldn't.

She helped me undress, helped wash my body and then powdered me down and helped me back into my pyjamas. I was totally dependent upon the nursing staff of the hospital for about four or five days. I didn't like it at all. For the bigger part of my life I had been in charge of what I did. I didn't really need help from anyone else but now things had changed. I was truly humbled.

My back surgery was not a success and I now suffer continual pain. I depend upon the doctors to provide me with pain-killing tablets. My wife drives me about in the car. Valerie even mows the lawn and does the gardening. I imagine most people don't like being dependent upon others, but I have become used to it and appreciate more and more the kindness shown to me.

Our God has told us that if we are not holy as he is holy we cannot enter the kingdom of heaven. Jesus, in the 'Sermon on the Mount', said to his listeners, 'Therefore you shall be perfect, just as your Father in heaven is perfect' (Matthew 5:48).

By ourselves none of us can be perfect as God is perfect. We can't save ourselves. And this truth hurts human pride. Humans like to think that somehow they can save themselves. Paul thought that being a good Pharisee would get him to heaven. Many people today believe that if they do the right thing, if they help other people and live by the 'golden rule', then God will save them. I've heard people say, 'Yes, I'll get to heaven. I've lived a good life. I've done the best I can.'

Nothing we can do will gain us a place in heaven. During my stay in hospital I was taught that I was dependent upon the work of the doctors and nurses. I couldn't help myself much at all. It is like that with salvation! You can't save yourself. As much as it might hurt your human pride, if you are to be saved you must go to the Lord Jesus Christ and trust yourself to him for salvation.

Jesus has told us that you must be perfect as God is perfect, if you are to enter heaven. You need the very perfection of God to be acceptable to God. And our text tells us that this is possible through faith in Jesus Christ. Our reading for today tells us the same truth (Philippians 3:9). When you trust in Jesus, his righteousness becomes your righteousness, and God looks at you through him. Speaking of the Lord Jesus Christ, Jeremiah the prophet calls him 'the LORD our Righteousness' (Jeremiah 23:6).

Reader, as I wrote before, you can't save yourself. Only Christ can do that. When the young nurse said to me, 'I'll wash you,' she spoke words that are spiritually true of what the Lord Jesus does for us. You can't wash away your sins. That is the work of the Lord Jesus Christ, and his alone.

Reader, have you trusted yourself to the one who is 'the Lord our Righteousness'?

Activities

1. What is meant by the biblical term 'justification'?
2. For what reason did the Pharisees think they would be saved?
3. How can a sinner be perfect in God's sight?
4. What is the 'golden rule'?

STORY 42

A valuable coat

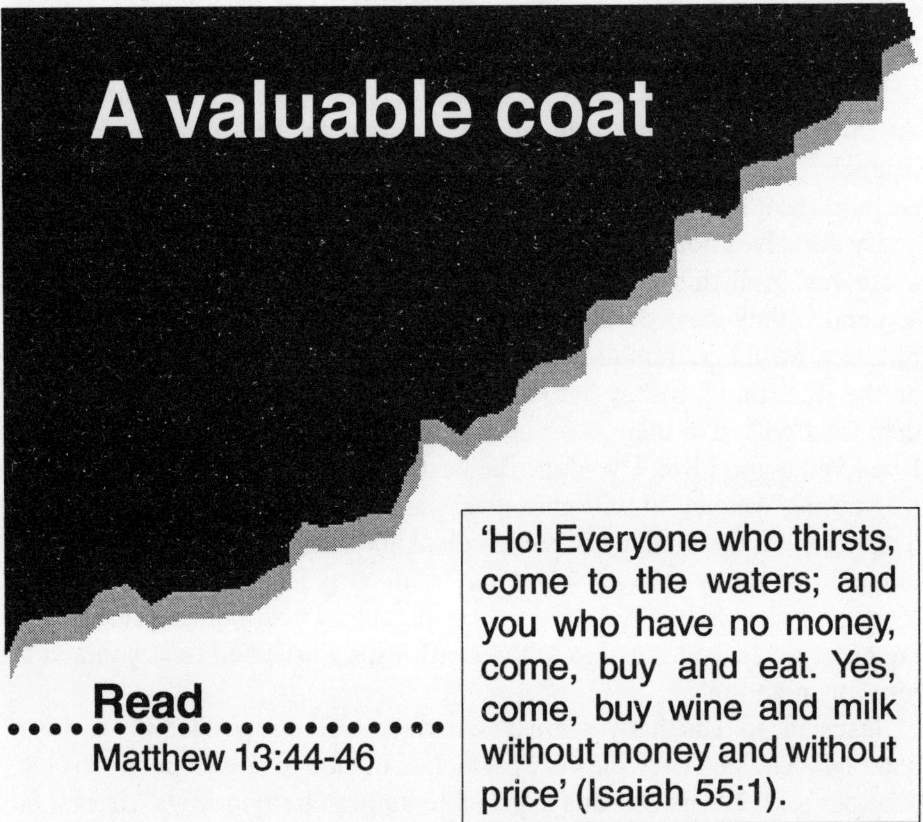

Read

Matthew 13:44-46

'Ho! Everyone who thirsts, come to the waters; and you who have no money, come, buy and eat. Yes, come, buy wine and milk without money and without price' (Isaiah 55:1).

One of the most valuable things in the world is the gospel of salvation. People hear the gospel daily over the radio, on the television, in books, in the newspaper and through the witness of Christians, but very few consider the saving work of Christ to be of any value.

Salvation is priceless. It cost the life of Jesus Christ, the Son of God, yet it is freely available to any sinner who sees his or her need. Our text for today is an invitation to sinners, from God himself, to come and drink from the wells of Christ's salvation.

Our reading tells us that this salvation is the pearl of great price that the man had to have. He was willing to do anything to get that pearl. It is wonderful to hear of someone who realizes that he or she is a sinner and does everything possible to find Christ as Saviour. But what is tragic is to have the pearl of salvation within your grasp and not realize that it is of value to you.

Some time ago a lady I know quite well showed me a small woman's jacket which she had purchased at a garage sale. I'm sure you have heard of garage sales, where people set up a stall in their garage and then try to sell all their old junk to other people who come along to buy (a bit like a car boot sale, but at their own homes). It is a great way to get rid of things that are not wanted any more.

This person, let's call her Elizabeth, stopped the car outside the place where the sale was taking place and went inside. She saw many bits and pieces, but what caught her eye was a small woman's jacket, which seemed to be made of some type of furred animal skin. There was a sign on it which read, '$20.00'.

Elizabeth looked at the jacket and said to the man who was selling the goods, 'I'll give you $10.00 for that jacket.' The man was very pleased to get rid of what he thought was another bit of rubbish, and Elizabeth took the jacket home. One of her grandchildren met her at the door, took the jacket and spent the afternoon playing with it. When Elizabeth's husband came home and saw the jacket, he picked it up and asked, 'Where did you get this?'

Elizabeth told him the story and her husband said, 'Don't let the kids play with it. I think it's valuable.'

Several days later the jacket was at a fur shop to be valued and the shop owner said, 'I'll give you $1,500.00 for that well-made fur jacket.' But Elizabeth had never had such a valuable jacket and so decided to keep it for herself.

Imagine how the original owner would have felt if he knew what he had sold for such a small amount of money. He had something that was worth a fortune and didn't know.

In our reading there is that short parable told by Jesus about the man who found a treasure hidden underground in another person's field. In the days of Jesus, people used to bury their valuables. There were no safes or strong banks to protect valuable possessions. The person who owned the field didn't know that in his field there was something worth a fortune. He sold his land and so lost a valuable treasure.

Reader, salvation is vital. Without being united to Christ your eternal destiny is hell. Christ and his salvation is so valuable that you should go to him to be saved. And that priceless salvation is yours just for the asking.

You should be willing to sacrifice all you have to obtain Christ as your Lord and Saviour. Salvation is more precious than gold or silver. It is more precious than anything the world might offer. Salvation is more precious than having a good time. It is more precious than sport, education, a big house and car and a nice family.

Don't be like the rich young ruler who went to Christ and asked what he needed to do to inherit eternal life. Jesus asked the young man to do one thing: 'Sell all that you have and distribute to the poor, and you will have treasure in heaven; and come, follow Me' (Luke 18:22). But that young man was rich and he loved his riches more than he wanted eternal life. How terrible!

Reader, what is first in your life?

Activities

1. What does salvation cost a sinner?
2. How did Jesus pay the price for the salvation of his people?
3. Name some of the things in your life that are important to you.
4. What should be the most important things in your life?

STORY 43

Timber!

Read

2 Samuel 7:12-17

'Behold, the Man whose name is the Branch! From His place He shall branch out, and He shall build the temple of the LORD' (Zechariah 6:12).

One of my cousins, Malcolm, lived on a farm about forty kilometres from our home. He lived well out in the bush, but I was able to visit his home quite often. I always looked forward to staying with Malcolm as his house was a most exciting place. There was no electricity and at night-time my aunty and uncle would light the lanterns which we would carry with us when we went from one room to another. There were some lanterns fixed in the rooms which were constantly used, such as the kitchen and dining-room.

Night-time was always an eerie time. The house was not far from some thick scrub and possums would get onto the roof of the house and scratch about making the most frightening sounds. If there was a thunderstorm I can still remember being terrified. The lightning would flash, the thunder would roar and the lantern would flicker in the breeze that blew under the door or through the windows.

But what made holidaying there even more exciting was that there was a trapdoor in one of the bedrooms — the one that Malcolm and I slept in — and that trapdoor led to a dungeon under the house. In that underground room there were some chains hanging from the walls, which were made of solid stone. I was soon to find out that the house had been built in the early days of the Australian settlement, and the room and chains under the house were for the several convicts who worked on the farm. Life with Malcolm was always exciting!

One day Uncle said that as we were strong young boys we could each take an axe and cut down trees in the scrub that stretched for miles. He told us that if the trees were too big for us to cut down, we could ringbark them. This meant we just cut out a ring of bark right around the tree so the sap that kept the tree alive could not move up the tree trunk. The tree then died. Malcolm and I worked very hard for several days, and slept well each night.

One day Aunty and Uncle went to town and Malcolm and I were left to look after the cows. But while the family was away we decided to get on with the job of ringbarking trees. Near the dairy, where the cows were milked, there were three huge gum trees that provided shade for the cattle. Well, Malcolm and I decided to ringbark those three trees. When Aunty and Uncle returned from their trip to town we proudly showed them our latest work. Malcolm's parents were not impressed, to say the least. The axes were put away and we were confined to the house for a while. The trees died and had to be cut down and new trees were planted beside the stumps. They came to nothing as the cows ate them very early in their life.

Several months later, out of the old stumps, there was new growth. Years later the cows were standing under the shade of the new trees which had grown from the old, dead-looking stumps. I imagine that now the new growth is as big as the original trees — maybe they are even taller than they were before they were cut down.

Our text for today refers to the Lord Jesus Christ as the 'Branch'. God made a wonderful promise to David. Through the prophet Nathan God said, 'Your kingdom shall be established for ever before you. Your throne shall be established for ever' (2 Samuel 7:16). Many years before Jesus was born the throne of David had come to an end. It was like a dead tree stump. But God's promise to David concerning his throne's endurance was to be fulfilled. Jesus, the 'Son of David', was a true descendant of David, and had the right to David's throne. So the kingdom of Jesus grew from the dead stump of David into a kingdom far greater than the world has ever known.

The Lord didn't come into this world as a great warrior, but as a baby — like the little shoot from the almost dead tree stump. When he rose from the grave, he ascended to heaven and sat upon the very throne of God as 'King of kings and Lord of lords' (Revelation 19:16). The kingdom of the Lord Jesus is greater than the kingdom of David as David's kingdom was simply the land of Israel. The kingdom of the Lord Jesus is worldwide and has citizens from the very beginning of human history.

The text continues to tell us that the one called the 'Branch' would build a temple. That temple is not one made of slabs of stone, but one constructed of saved people. Together the saints are the temple of God. Our next story will teach you something about that temple.

Every time you pass a tree stump, have a close look to see if there are any branches sprouting out of what looks dead and worthless. Every time you do, think of Jesus Christ, who has fulfilled the promise that God made to King David, that his throne would be an everlasting throne.

And, reader, are you a servant and lover of the 'Branch'?

Activities

1. Why should Jesus Christ be called 'the Branch'?
2. Why is Jesus called 'Son of David'?
3. Why is Jesus called 'King of kings and Lord of lords'?
4. Where do we find the kingdom of God today?

STORY 44

I'm a brick!

Read

2 Chronicles 6:1-11

'Now therefore, you are no longer strangers and foreigners, but fellow citizens with the saints and members of the household of God, having been built on the foundation of the apostles and prophets, Jesus Christ Himself being the chief cornerstone, in whom the whole building, being joined together, grows into a holy temple in the Lord, in whom you also are being built together for a habitation of God in the Spirit' (Ephesians 2:19-22).

It's hard to believe that Christians are part of the building material of a temple, but the Bible tells us that this is so. Just read the text for today and you will see that, together, God's people make up the true temple.

Now one of the most exciting events in a person's life is when the decision is made to build a house in which to live. The home my wife and I live in was built some years ago and we put a lot of effort into planning a home that would suit us when I had to give up work.

At that time I was a pastor of a congregation, but Valerie and I decided we should build a house, just in case it was needed. We decided to build in a small country town where we had lived for many years. After some searching we found what we thought was the smallest plot of land and bought it. We wanted a small plot so there would not be much lawn to mow when we were old.

We planned our home with an en-suite beside the bedroom as this would be helpful in old age. We made sure that the light switches were beside the bed, as well as the switch that controlled the electric fan on the ceiling. We have no steps into the house and we think we have planned things well.

After the plans were drawn up, we approached a builder, who was an elder in a nearby congregation, and asked if he would build our house. He said he was retiring, but as we weren't in a hurry to have the house built, he would do the work. It took him about three years to build the house and we are very happy with what we have. God has been very good to us.

After the excitement of drawing up the plans of the house, the builder told us to select the bricks we would like. Now picking the bricks was one of the most difficult jobs my wife and I had. I liked darker-coloured bricks with a fleck in them, while my wife liked lighter-coloured bricks. We spent many hours visiting brickworks, looking at many types of brick. We couldn't agree for many weeks about what we wanted, but eventually made our choice. We both had to give way a little, but now we are very happy with our choice.

We visited the building of the house many times and I was very interested in the bricklaying. It seemed so simple. At last I asked the bricklayer if I could have a go. He laughed at me and said, 'All right. Let's see you make a mess of things!'

The result was that I couldn't lay a brick properly. The brickie said, 'I think you ought to try and build a barbecue. That's about your level.' I tried hard, but eventually had to get the brickie to build the barbecue.

The house was eventually completed and as it happened, due to injury, I was forced to retire early and now we live in the house we expected to occupy fifteen years later. You see how good God is! He planned that we should have that house ready when it was needed years before we had planned.

We see about us many buildings. Some are well constructed but others last only a short time. In the reading for today, you will have read about King Solomon building a temple to be used for the worship of God. It was built exactly according to the plans God had given him. That temple must have been a glorious building. But Solomon's temple was a symbol of the perfect temple being built by God, that is, the spiritual temple being made

Do you really think *you* could lay a brick?

up of God's people from all ages. The Scriptures liken the church to a human building.

First there is the foundation made up of the apostles and prophets. The glorious 'cornerstone' is the Lord Jesus himself. The apostle Peter tells us this great truth when he writes, 'Behold, I lay in Zion a chief cornerstone, elect, precious, and he who believes on Him will by no means be put to shame' (1 Peter 2:6).

Then on top of the foundation the bricks are put into place. This building commenced with the first saint found upon the earth. The temple will be completed when the last saint is brought to faith in Christ. And when that happens our Saviour will return again.

This spiritual temple, then, is the whole body of believers who are born again of God's Holy Spirit. And this crowd of believers will ever offer to God spiritual sacrifices through the one and only Mediator, Jesus Christ. We shall praise God and serve him for ever.

The Lord Jesus went to his people, Israel, to tell them of the great salvation that was to be found in him. But the nation wanted nothing to do with Jesus and the leaders of Israel had the Son of God crucified. They rejected the 'chief cornerstone' and God punished the nation for their terrible sin.

Reader, what about you? Are you one of those living stones which help make up the true temple of God? You are if you are born again — if you trust in Jesus Christ alone for your salvation, and have repented of your sins. But if you are not one of those bricks in the spiritual temple then beware, for Jesus said of himself, as the 'chief cornerstone': 'On whomever it falls, it will grind him to powder' (Luke 20:18).

Activities

1. What is a temple?
2. Of what is the temple of God constructed?
3. Who dwells in the temple of God?
4. What is a 'cornerstone'? What was the use of a 'cornerstone'? In what way is Jesus the 'chief cornerstone' of God's temple?

STORY 45

I don't think much of that!

Read

Revelation 22:1-7

> 'Finally, there is laid up for me the crown of righteousness, which the Lord, the righteous Judge, will give to me on that Day, and not to me only but also to all who have loved his appearing' (2 Timothy 4:8).

The apostle Paul was a great missionary. He travelled far and wide to preach the good news that Jesus, the Christ, had come to save sinners. Paul had been whipped by cruel, godless people, he had been thrown into prison, he had been shipwrecked — he had suffered so much serving the Lord. But he knew that at the end of life there was a 'crown of righteousness' waiting for him — and not just for him, but for all who love the Lord Jesus Christ. Even though we do not deserve any reward, God does reward his people in a most wonderful way for their faithfulness.

I still remember my Uncle Norman, who loved to spend time in our boat on the river that flowed beside our farm. He would push the boat out from the river-bank, drop the anchor in the middle of the river and fish for hours. He usually had a book to read and didn't really mind whether he caught anything or not.

One day he asked me if I would like to go fishing with him. I was always ready to go fishing, so gathered my gear together and walked down to the river. He had decided to use the boat, but when we reached the river, the tide was low and the boat was high and dry on the river-bank. Between the boat and the river there was a strip of mud about three metres wide.

Uncle Norman said he would push the boat out into the river and then bring it back so I could hop in without getting dirty. That suited me as I didn't want to walk through the filthy mud. But as my uncle was pushing the boat across the mud flat, the boat suddenly slipped across the muddy stretch. Uncle Norman was not going to let the boat go, so hung on tightly. He fell over and the sliding boat dragged him on his stomach through the mud. I began to laugh, particularly when he went to stand up in the river beside the boat and disappeared under water. He found out that the river was very deep in that particular spot.

Before Uncle Norman went home he suggested that I might like to send him a drawing of what he looked like when he fell into the mud. He also said he would send me a reward for doing such a drawing. I was about ten years of age at that time and soon had a sketch done. I thought it was a really good illustration. Mum posted a letter and the sketch to dear old Uncle Norman.

Several days later there was a letter in the post for me. I knew it was from Uncle Norman and I excitedly opened the envelope wanting to find out what he had sent me for my drawing. There was a letter and I could feel something wrapped up in the page. I opened the page and to my disappointment a heap of stamps fell on the floor. I looked at them and then at the letter. The letter praised me for my drawing and said that the stamps were my reward for such a fine sketch.

I was thoroughly disappointed. What good were stamps to a ten-year-old boy? I thought Uncle Norman had cheated me out of what should have been something worthwhile.

Our text for today teaches us that God rewards all of his faithful people. And God's rewards will never disappoint. Good things are in store for the saints. Eternal life is ours, in the new heavens and earth. We shall live with Jesus and all the other saints. In that home there will be no sin, no death, no tears, no pain — just everlasting joy in the presence of Christ. Our reading for today gives us a picture of some of the wonders that await all who love Jesus. Paul said he looked forward to that 'crown of righteousness' which Christ would give him on the great Day of Judgement.

Reader, if you are a Christian, you can say the same. All of God's people have something really wonderful to look forward to. None of God's rewards will cause disappointment!

Activities

1. What is 'the crown of righteousness' spoken about in our text?
2. Why should God reward the saints?
3. Name some of the wonderful things that await the saints.

STORY 46

Boo!

Read

Mark 12:13-17

'Beware of the leaven of the Pharisees, which is hypocrisy. For there is nothing covered that will not be revealed, nor hidden that will not be known' (Luke 12:1-2).

A hypocrite is a person who pretends to be something he or she is not. In ancient Rome and Greece actors were called hypocrites, because they usually wore a mask in the play, pretending to be another person. It's easy to see how we have come to use the word to describe people who give the impression they have a different character to what they really have.

Many times I've seen people wearing masks, and children enjoy making masks they can use in their play. In fact you can buy very good masks today. I have a rubber one, which I've had for many years. My children hated it when they were young. And now my grandchildren hate it too. In fact one day when I put it over my face, one of the grandchildren was terrified and began to cry. Valerie decided the mask had caused enough problems and for several years I couldn't find where she had hidden it.

When I was a schoolteacher I used to travel to monthly meetings in Sydney. I was a representative of the local teachers at the union for teachers. I would leave in the car early on Saturday morning and return home late Saturday night. I didn't like driving in Sydney and was pleased when someone else took over my task of attending the meetings.

One Saturday, at lunchtime, I decided to walk about the city near the conference area and came to a shop that sold 'magic' bits and pieces. There were many tricks that people could buy, and I've always enjoyed a joke, so I went in and had a look around. Then I spotted one of the best masks I had ever seen. There was some red hair on the head, ugly-looking eyes, the mouth was twisted up and two teeth could be seen between the lips. It looked terrible, so I bought it. I carried it around with me in a bag and every now and again had a look at it and began to smile. I thought that I would scare Valerie with it when I arrived home late at night.

The meeting finished and soon I was on my way home, smiling every now and again when I thought of frightening my wife. I was very quiet when I walked up the steps into our home and then put on the mask. It looked hideous. I turned the hall light on and went into the bedroom where Valerie was waking up.

'Is that you, Jim?' she asked.

I just grunted a little and moved close to the bed. Then Valerie turned the light on and looked. I think people many miles away heard her scream that night. I very quickly took the mask off and began to say how sorry I was to scare her. Valerie was upset with my prank, and I couldn't find the mask for many months after that. But that mask made me out to be something I was not. I was like the true hypocrite of two thousand years ago.

In our text for today, Jesus said that the Pharisees were hypocrites. They pretended to be godly people, but really they hated Jesus, the Son of God. The people of Israel thought they were godly people. They wore their religious masks very well. But Jesus could see through their pretence. He could see their sinful, hating hearts. He knew they weren't God's people, but rather belonged to Satan.

In the reading for today you should have noticed how the Pharisees and Herodians pretended to be interested in what Christ had to say. They even said of Jesus that he taught 'the way of God in truth' (Mark 12:14). But they didn't believe what they said. They were trying to trap Jesus into saying something they could use to prove he was not the Christ of God. They were hypocrites! Jesus could not be trapped by these sinful men.

Now, you are warned about hypocrisy. It is so easy to pretend that you are religious. You may possibly go to Sunday School and church. You might even read your Bible and pray. You might let people think that you are on your way to heaven. But really you don't like what you are doing. You would rather be out with your godless friends and you can't wait until you leave home so you can do as you please. But still you pretend to be something you are not.

Jesus can see through your mask. He knows the thoughts of your heart. Reader, if you are a hypocrite, then repent of your sin and ask for forgiveness. Then with a true heart, and a love for the things of God, serve the Lord Jesus with all your heart, soul, mind and body.

Activities

1. Why are some people scared of the dark?
2. What is a hypocrite? Are you a religious hypocrite?
3. In what way were the Pharisees hypocrites?

STORY 47

Danger at sea

Read

1 Samuel 24:1-15

'When Gentiles, who do not have the law, by nature do the things contained in the law, these, although not having the law, are a law to themselves, who show the work of the law written in their hearts, their conscience also bearing witness, and between themselves their thoughts accusing or else excusing them...' (Romans 2:14-15).

Fishing at sea is the place to catch the big ones. When I bought my first boat for outside fishing, I made up some rules that I used to decide whether I went out to sea or not.

First of all, the weather had to be basically fine. The wind forecast was to be for winds of not more than fifteen knots and the waves were to be small enough to launch the boat on the beach and get out to the ocean. Fishing was done on Saturdays except during the school holidays. If I was planning a trip out to sea, I would always drive to the beach on Friday afternoon and check the size of the waves. Then if all the conditions were right I would get the boat ready for an early morning start.

I had arranged a trip out to sea, and much to my disappointment the forecast announced on Friday warned of strong winds. So I rang my fishing friend and said, 'You can sleep in tomorrow. The forecast is not good and it's not worth the risk going out.'

But my friend was very disappointed and in my heart I really wanted to get out on the ocean. I set the alarm clock for a very early hour with the aim of checking the accuracy of the forecast at about two o'clock in the morning. I thought it was possible that a mistake had been made.

When the alarm rang I turned the radio on and again heard the forecast which gave the same report as the night before — there was a strong wind warning. I got out of bed and walked outside. There was not a movement of air and as I went back to bed, I thought to myself, 'Maybe we could have a couple of hours on the ocean before the wind gets up.'

I woke again a couple of hours later and again checked the weather outside the house. Everything was calm. I felt sure the forecaster had made an error about the wind speed, so I rang my fishing friend and asked him if he wanted to spend some time on the ocean. He was very happy to do so.

When we reached the beach, the waves were very small and there was no wind blowing at all. A few surfboard riders were on the ocean and we could see their fire blazing back on the headland. The smoke from the fire was wafting straight up into the sky.

Before long we were out at sea, fishing away, without a care in the world. The wind was calm and I began to think the forecaster had made a great mistake about the weather.

We were about six kilometres from the shore when we noticed the smoke from the surfboard riders' fire flattening out and blowing in our direction. I had the sudden thought that the strong wind had hit the beach area and before long would be blowing where we were. I said to my friend, 'Look at the smoke back at the beach. The wind is coming. Let's get our lines up and get back to the beach.' But before we could get in our lines the wind hit us. The ocean went from calm to waves two metres high within a few seconds. We began to slowly make our way back to the shore which seemed so far away. The wind was roaring and the waves were smashing into my small boat.

Very slowly the shore was getting closer. Then without warning I noticed that water was beginning to flood into the boat. The continual smashing of the waves into the boat had caused the keel to begin to split apart. I began to feel very uncomfortable. I now knew that I should have taken notice of the forecast.

My friend stuffed some cloth into the split and I began to bail the rising sea water out of the boat. The beach began to look further and further away and I knew that I had no hope of swimming that far. I began to think I might drown. But we kept bailing and after an hour or so the waves lessened as we neared the shore.

When we reached the shore, I said, 'I will always take notice of the forecast in future — even if everything seems to indicate that it is wrong.'

I was so frightened by the near drowning, I sold my boat. However, some months later I purchased another one — only a little bigger and more able to stand up to the waves.

Our text for today speaks about our conscience. Your conscience is the small voice that tells you what is right and wrong. It is like the forecast which I ignored. If your conscience warns you that what you are about to do is wrong, then obey it. If your conscience tells you that you have done something wrong, then confess your sin to the Lord.

Our reading for today speaks of David, who cut the corner off King Saul's robe while he slept. In verse 5 we read that this action of David's troubled his heart. His conscience told him that he should not have done this to the king. He made sure that his servants did King Saul no harm.

As you read more of the Bible, God's law will become very important to you and your conscience will be an even better guide to what you should or should not do.

Reader, you need to remember the words of Jiminy Cricket, who said that you should always let your conscience be your guide. This is good advice. But allow your conscience to be trained by the Word of God.

Activities

1. What is a 'conscience'?
2. Why should you obey your conscience?
3. How can a Christian train his or her conscience?
4. Why was David's conscience disturbed by what he did to King Saul's clothing?

STORY 48

Take up your cross

> 'And he who does not take his cross and follow after Me is not worthy of Me' (Matthew 10:38).

Read

Matthew 27:27-37

Read your Bible reading for today and think about the death of Jesus Christ. We can never really understand how much he suffered on behalf of his people. The Roman soldiers were very cruel in the way they treated their prisoners. Jesus suffered greatly at the hands of those cruel men. But when Jesus suffered, he also suffered the anger of God because he was bearing the sins of his people. And God hates sin.

Jesus was told to take up his cross and carry it down to the place of execution. The Bible tells us that Jesus was so weak after being whipped and tormented, that he couldn't carry the cross. So a man named Simon (Matthew 27:32) was forced to carry Christ's cross.

Now if anyone in those days was told to take up his cross, it meant that at the end of the road he would be nailed to that cross and eventually die. And the death of the cross was a very cruel death. Sometimes it took the men and women nailed to the cross many hours to die. Trying to live a little longer, the crucified person would push his body up so he could get a better breath of air. At the end of the day, if the person on the cross was still alive the Romans would sometimes break his legs, and then he would quickly die as he could not breathe properly. Death on the cross was so horrible and degrading that no Roman citizen was crucified.

Our text then contains words that do not appeal to us. Jesus was speaking to the disciples, and what he said to them applies to all who are Christians. We are told to take up our cross and follow Jesus. If we are not willing to do so, then Jesus says we are not worthy of him. The way of the

'The Burning of Bishop Hooper'
from J. C. Ryle, *Light from Old Times.* Chas. J. Thynne, London, 1902

cross meant death, so Jesus requires of all who follow him that they be ready, if need be, to lay down their life for him. We are to love Jesus more than anything we own — even more than our lives. Now, can you say that you are willing to sacrifice everything you own for Jesus?

When we open our Bible and our history books we find the names of many who sacrificed so much for their Saviour. Many people have willingly laid down their lives for the sake of Christ.

One such man was Bishop Hooper. He lived in the sixteenth century and was a faithful follower of Christ. He showed great love to the people, but when Mary became Queen of England she had Bishop Hooper arrested. Mary was a Roman Catholic queen and hated those who were true followers of Christ. Hooper was sent to jail and after much questioning was sentenced to death. The death penalty he was to suffer was being burned at the stake.

Before Hooper was taken to the place of execution he was asked to change his beliefs and he would be set free. He was told, 'Consider that life is sweet, and death is bitter. Therefore seeing life may be had for the asking, consent to live...'

But Hooper replied, 'True ... death is bitter and life is sweet; but, alas! consider that the death to come is more bitter, and the life to come is more sweet.'[1] Bishop Hooper longed to be with Christ. That was all that really mattered. He knew that Christ loved him, so how could he deny the one who had saved him?

Hooper was taken to the place of execution, tied to a stake and the fire was set alight. Earnestly Bishop Hooper prayed to God for strength to die bravely. He forgave all who had plotted his death and for almost forty-five minutes he suffered terribly in the flames. But true to his word, God gave him the grace he needed to die bravely.

Here was a man who was willing to take up his cross and follow Jesus. He willingly laid down his life in the service of his Master. He had spent many years preaching the gospel and winning people to faith in Jesus. If you are a Christian, you will one day have the opportunity to meet this great saint.

So are you willing to daily take up your cross and follow Jesus? This means that each day of your life you make the commitment to be faithful to Jesus, no matter what. If someone pokes fun at you because you don't become involved in swearing, telling lies, stealing or the many other sinful things that people do, then so be it. You must be willing to lose your old friends who no longer like you because you are now a Christian. You must be willing, if called to do so, to even lay down your life for the sake of Jesus, who loves you.

The verse which follows our text for today reads: 'He who finds his life will lose it, and he who loses his life for My sake will find it' (Matthew 10:39). To save your earthly life by denying Christ means you will lose eternal life with Christ. To lose your earthly life because you love Christ means you will find eternal life in the presence of your Saviour.

Reader, what is your situation today? Are you willing to take up your cross and follow Jesus? I pray that this is so!

Activities

1. List some of the crosses that Christians carry daily?
2. List some sacrifices you have made for Jesus' sake.
3. What sacrifice did Jesus make for his people?

[1]1. John Foxe, *Foxe's Book of Martyrs,* Moody Press, U.S.A., p.435

STORY 49

It's your boat!

Read
Genesis 3:1-9

'They shall bear their iniquity' (Ezekiel 44:10).

We live in a world where people don't like to accept the responsibility for what they do wrong. So many times we read of people breaking the law and then blaming someone else for what they did. They will say their mum and dad didn't look after them properly, or claim that society did not give them a fair go — everyone is to blame but themselves. But the fact remains that each of us is responsible for what we do, whether good or bad.

When Eve sinned she blamed Satan. When Adam sinned he blamed God for giving him a wife, who led him astray. But God punished them both because they were responsible for their own sins. Read your Bible passage for today and you will learn that all are responsible for their own sins.

Our text also teaches that when God's people began to worship idols, he held them responsible for their sin — no one else was to blame for what they did. So we need to be very careful in all our doings, as one day we shall have to give an account to God for all that we have done. We shall not be able to blame someone else, but God will hold us personally responsible.

In our daily life we are responsible for our actions, and sometimes suffer for what we do.

My brother John and I used to go fishing together. We both enjoyed going out to sea trying to catch the big ones. And many times we did catch them. But getting out to sea was not always easy. We would have to prepare the boat and make sure the outboard engine was working perfectly. We would travel to the beach the evening before to make sure the waves weren't too big. We had to prepare our fishing gear. But one difficult thing was getting up early in the morning to get the boat down to the beach or the river. Sometimes we launched the boat into the river and went out to sea over the bar at the mouth of the river. Getting up early, well before sunrise, was especially difficult in winter. Sometimes the frost would be on the ground and we would be forced to wear thick woollen clothes.

One winter morning we were out of bed early, had a warm breakfast and soon had the boat down to the launching ramp in the river. The slight breeze blowing was very chilly and I hoped we could launch the boat and get into it without having to take our shoes off. We could do this if we were careful and pulled the boat back beside the launching ramp.

I backed the trailer down into the river and hopped out of the car, ready to slide the boat off the trailer and into the water. John and I had done this many times and usually he would hang onto the rope attached to the boat, ready to prevent the boat drifting too far out into the river. He would then pull the boat back in to the shore.

I didn't say anything to John, but just assumed he would be holding the rope as I pushed the boat off the trailer. The boat slid gently into the river. As the boat floated away from the shore, I said, 'John, you can pull the boat in while I park the car off the road.'

But John simply looked at me and said, 'How can I pull the boat in? I wasn't holding the rope. You didn't tell me you were ready to launch.'

I looked through the darkness to see the boat drifting away from the river-bank and downstream. 'It's your fault,' I said to John, 'you should have been holding the rope. You can dive into the water and swim out to get the boat.'

But John simply replied, 'I'm not to blame. Anyway, it's your boat. Enjoy the swim!'

It was dark and very cold as I stripped off and plunged into the freezing water. I swam for the boat and was soon starting the motor. My whole body seemed frozen. My teeth were chattering as the boat nosed into the shore. John threw our gear into the boat and as we made our way down to the entrance to the ocean, I dressed in my warm clothes.

Regardless of how I felt, I knew that I was to blame for the mishap. I hadn't told John what I was doing and even though I thought he should have been holding the rope, I could only blame myself.

Each one of us is responsible for our sins. We shall have to answer to God for what we have done. No one will be to blame for your sins, but you! Others may have influenced you to sin, Satan may have tempted you, but you are responsible for what you have done.

Isn't it a wonderful truth that Jesus was willing to lift the sins of his people from each one of them and bear them himself? (see Isaiah 53:12 and 1 Peter 2:24). Jesus became sin for us before his heavenly Father. As the Sin-bearer he was punished by God in the place of his people so that his people would be forgiven.

Reader, ask the Lord to give you the spirit of repentance that you may stand before the judgement seat of Christ cleansed of your sins and clothed in the righteousness of your Saviour.

Activities

1. Why do so many people blame others for what they do wrong?
2. Who did Adam blame for his sin?
3. Who is to blame for your sins? Why did you give that answer?

STORY 50

A broken window

'He has not dealt with us according to our sins, nor punished us according to our iniquities' (Psalm 103:10).

Read

Revelation 11:15-18

In the Bible we read again and again about the grace of God. I would like to tell you a story that explains what is meant by the word 'grace'.

In my younger days I really enjoyed a game of cricket. It was great standing out in the sun batting and bowling and generally having a good time. On the farm there was always plenty of room and no one had to worry about hitting a ball through a window. But one problem with playing cricket at home when I was young was the shortage of players. Many times it was just John and I — and the dog. The stumps were set up beside the fowl house and the batsman became the wicket-keeper as well. The ball would thump into the fowl house and upset the chickens, but would go no further. The bowler was the only fielder. Still we enjoyed our game. Sometimes some local boys would come over and we'd have half a dozen to play — three on each side.

But one afternoon, John and I were invited to have a game of cricket in town after school. We were to play in a small paddock and there were quite a few children ready to play. The last thing the lady of the house said as we were going out the gate was: 'Now be careful and don't break any windows!' I didn't think it possible to break a window playing cricket. Such a thing never happened on the farm.

Soon we settled down to a very enjoyable game. It was great having so many children to play with! When it was my turn to bat, I hit one ball as hard as I could. It flew through the air and over a fence. Then we heard the smashing sound of a window breaking. We grabbed the cricket gear and ran for our lives.

That night I had a guilty conscience. I knew I should have owned up to what I had done. I should have gone and spoken to the lady who lived in the house and told her I was to blame.

The next morning at school, we were laughing about our cricket game and what had happened. But I felt very uneasy about the incident. Then at the assembly the school principal stood up and told everyone that he had had a phone call from a woman whose window had been broken by some children playing cricket. She knew the name of one boy because it had been written on the ball that had smashed her window. Now the school principal wanted to see all of the cricketers in his office.

My heart started to tremble. I knew I was in trouble. In the office I owned up to what I had done. The principal was not very happy with me and told me that I was to visit the lady on my way home from school.

I was trembling when I knocked on the lady's door. When she opened the door all I could say was, 'I'm sorry.' The lady then told me to come inside. She showed me the window that had been broken. It had been repaired by then. 'I know your mum and dad. They'll be disappointed with you, young Jimmie. However I think we can work things out, without telling them what you did,' Mrs Campbell said. 'For the next week, after school, you can call in and do some gardening — fifteen minutes each day.'

I was very relieved and for the next five afternoons on the way home from school I spent some time cleaning up Mrs Campbell's garden. At the end of the week, Mrs Campbell came to me and said, 'You've done a good job, Jimmie. Now I'd like you to have this for the work you've done.'

With that she handed me a two-shilling coin. Back then that was a lot of money. All I could say was, 'I don't deserve it, but thanks very much.'

That's what 'grace' is. I deserved a good smacking for my actions. (If Mum and Dad had found out I would most likely have had a strap around the legs, but no one told them about the incident.) But instead I was given something I did not deserve — I was given two shillings.

The Bible tells us plainly that the wages of sin is death (Romans 6:23). I am a sinner and deserve death — eternal hell. But God has been good to me. He has given me faith in his Son, Jesus Christ. He has washed away my sins. I know that I have done nothing to deserve such a blessing. To show my love for Jesus, with God's help, I try to obey his commandments. I try to live a holy life. And when my life comes to an end and I look back over the things I have done serving Christ, all I will be able to say, with all the other saints, is: 'We have done what was our duty to do' (Luke 17:10).

We deserve no reward from God for doing only what we should have done, but the Bible tells us again and again that God will reward us for being faithful. Even though we deserve his anger, we shall receive his love and be blessed greatly.

Our reading for today contains words of praise to God, and part of that praise says: 'You should reward Your servants the prophets and the saints, and those who fear Your name, small and great...' (Revelation 11:18). What a wonderful and gracious God we have!

Reader, can you praise the Lord for his wonderful grace in your life? If you are a Christian you know the grace of God. Heaven is yours, when your sins should have taken you to hell. Always thank God for his goodness to you.

Activities

1. What is meant by the biblical word 'grace'?
2. What does the Bible tell us is the wages of sin? What does this mean?
3. Why should God give a Christian any reward?

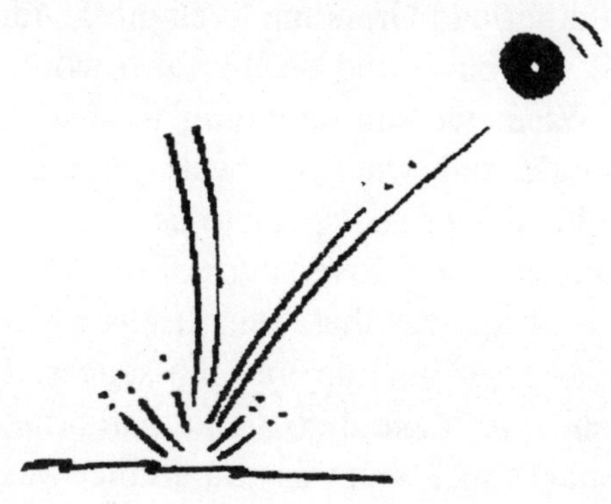

STORY 51

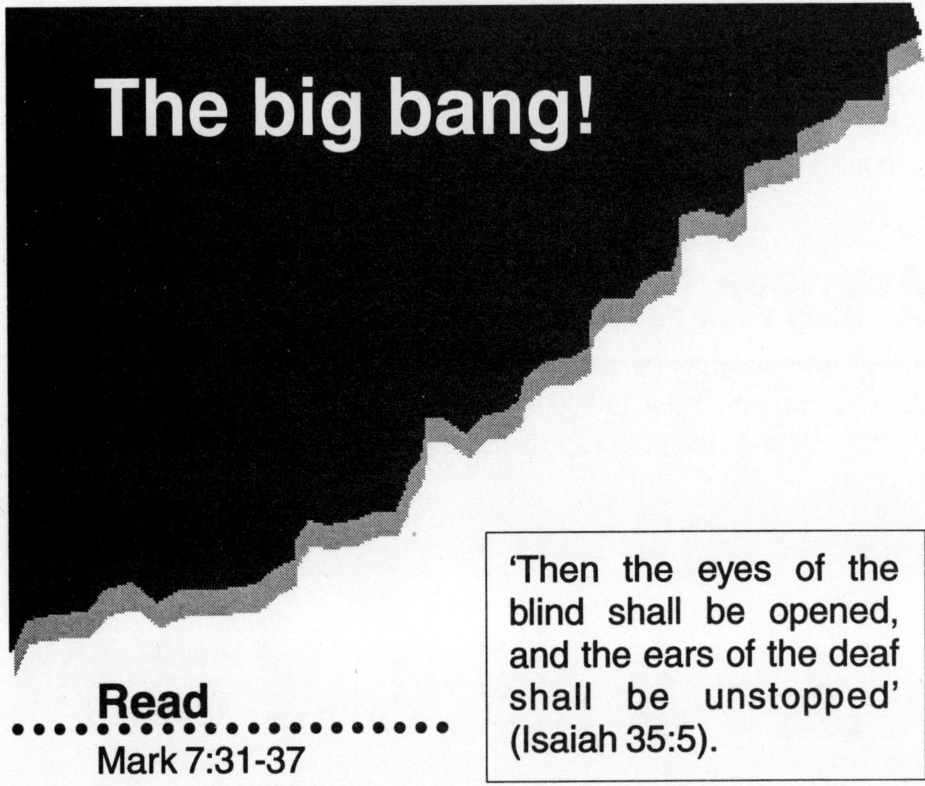

The big bang!

Read

Mark 7:31-37

'Then the eyes of the blind shall be opened, and the ears of the deaf shall be unstopped' (Isaiah 35:5).

Being deaf is a real burden. Every now and again my wife tells me I must be deaf as she calls me to help with the washing of the dishes and I never seem to hear. I'm sure many of my readers suffer from this type of deafness. Many times you hear only those things you want to hear.

My dad had a hearing aid and his father, my grandfather, was totally deaf. This grandfather I can remember well, even though he died when I was about ten years old. Grandfather and Grandma lived on the farm with Mum and Dad. He helped milk the cows and do the farm work. But he couldn't hear a word spoken. When we said anything we had to speak looking at Grandfather. He could tell what we were saying just by watching our lips. Then he would answer and speak to us.

Grandfather had a bushy moustache and loved cups of tea. One special thing I remember about his cups of tea was that many times when the tea was hot, he would pour the tea out of his cup into the saucer. Then he would blow on the tea in the saucer to make it cool and then drink the tea out of the saucer. Another unusual thing about this grandfather was that he liked tobacco. He didn't smoke cigarettes or have a pipe, but he had what was called 'plug tobacco'. Plug tobacco was a solid block of tobacco. It was very hard. He would cut off a small piece of the tobacco and then chew it up. The tobacco stained his bushy moustache. He used to tell my brother John and me many funny stories. He was a Christian and also told us many Bible stories as well.

One day as John and I were walking along with Grandfather the dog barked very loudly. Grandfather turned around and said, 'Rusty, be quiet. I heard you!' John and I were amazed as we thought Grandfather could not hear anything. But he said that he heard the dog barking.

That afternoon John and I decided we would find out for sure if Grandfather could hear things or not. We stood behind him and shouted out. We clapped our hands, but he didn't move. Mum and Dad asked what we were doing, so we told them about the dog barking and that Grandfather had heard the dog. Mum and Dad said that was impossible as Grandfather had been totally deaf for many years.

Well, John and I decided to put Grandfather to the test. When we went to school the next day, we went to a shop that sold fireworks and bought a couple of the biggest bangers that we could. We planned to explode them behind Grandfather and see what happened.

That afternoon, after milking was finished, Grandfather was chipping the weeds in the garden, when John and I struck our matches and lit the fuses of the bangers. We just stood and watched Grandfather. The two bangers made a tremendous noise, and sure enough Grandfather jumped around quickly. He looked at us and the puffs of smoke that were rising from the ground and said, 'You little tigers. You frightened the life out of me!' So we had proved that Grandfather could hear some things.

Our text tells us that one of the miracles Jesus would perform was to give hearing to the deaf. Our Bible reading is of a deaf man who was

healed by Jesus. This truly was an amazing miracle. But the Bible also tells us of people who are spiritually deaf. Jesus spoke of people who had good hearing, yet could not understand what he was saying. Paul, writing to the Romans, spoke of sinful people who simply could not understand spiritual matters.

Now God calls sinners to repentance. Ministers preach the way of salvation and some people are converted in worship and believe in Christ. Sometimes God's Spirit quietly convicts sinners of their sins as they are walking down the street. Then there are times when there is a death, and people begin to think about their own death and the judgement which is to follow. God's Spirit is calling a little louder to sinners in this situation.

A man in my congregation had drifted away from Christ and was living for himself. One day he was driving his four-wheel-drive car along the highway, when a semi-trailer hit his vehicle. He was very badly injured and for some time the doctors weren't sure whether he would survive the accident or not. But God was very gracious and Donald survived. Today he walks with a limp. He has to use a walking stick to get about, but he is happy to tell everyone that the accident was God's way of shouting to him that he needed to repent of his sins and return to Jesus for his salvation. Donald also says that every pain he experiences causes him to thank God for his love and great mercy in saving him from hell.

God will enable his people to hear his call. Sometimes the call of the Holy Spirit is very quiet and some people listen and believe. Sometimes, God uses the big bang to bring people to their senses, that they might believe and be saved.

Reader, has the Holy Spirit spoken to you, through the reading of the Bible, through the preaching of the Word, through some incident that has happened, and called you to repentance? If you are one of God's people you will hear the Holy Spirit calling you to repentance and faith. And when the Spirit calls you, then ask God to take over your life so that you might love and serve the Lord Jesus for ever.

Activities

1. What is meant by the word *'Ephphatha'* which Jesus used? (Look again at today's Bible reading if you don't know.)
2. What miracle did Jesus perform that is recorded in your reading for today?
3. What does God do that makes it possible for spiritually deaf people to hear the gospel call? Have you heard the gospel call? How have you responded?

STORY 52

Odd one out!

Read

Galatians 5:16-26

'For this is the message that you heard from the beginning, that we should love one another' (1 John 3:11).

Well, we have come to the end of fifty-two stories and their teachings. Do you remember the story of blind Bartimaeus (chapter 31), who took the one opportunity he had to be healed. I told you that you should not put off the day of your salvation, because you might not have another day.

You have now come to the end of this book and what is your relationship with Jesus? Is he now your Lord and Saviour? Or will you put this book down and forget all that has been written? If you are a Christian you should be a different person from what you were before. You will be a lover of Jesus Christ — and you will love all your brothers and sisters in Christ with special affection. You will also even love your enemies.

The great mark of a Christian is love of God and love of your fellow man and woman. Christians are called to be different from the ordinary people of this world. Are you different? Do others recognize that you are a Christian, just by the way you live? That should be the case.

Some years ago my wife and I, with two of our daughters, made a trip to Singapore. We had spent some days in Hong Kong and really enjoyed the different way of life in that large city. Then we flew to Singapore for a five-day stay. It was again very exciting to be in a city that was so different from the cities of Australia. In Singapore we met other Australians and even met several people who knew my brother John, back in Australia.

I wanted to have some silk shirts made and when I asked a tailor to make some he asked me what was my occupation. I told him he wouldn't understand what I was talking about, but he said, 'Tell me!'

I told him I was a Presbyterian minister. The man grabbed my hand, threw his arms around me and told me that he was a Christian too. We talked about our love for Jesus and then he said he would make shirts for me very cheaply. This he did and they are still wearing well ten years later.

We visited many places of interest in Singapore and we were always surrounded by many other tourists. At one place of interest a bus pulled up and thirty or forty Japanese tourists, well prepared with cameras, got off. They all had shiny, jet black hair and we noticed that our Lisa, who has blonde hair, stood out in the crowd. Suddenly several of the Japanese tourists ran over to Lisa and beckoned her to come with them. They were pointing at her hair and then touching their own. They wanted Lisa to stand with them and have a photo taken. So there stood Lisa between some black-haired tourists and she had her photo taken quite a few times. I sometimes think that somewhere in Japan today, someone is showing the photos taken when they visited Singapore and there is our blonde-headed Lisa for all to see. Because of her hair colour Lisa stood out in the crowd. For this reason she was different from the rest.

This is how it should be with Christians. We are called to be different, when we become a follower of Christ. The Bible tells us that when we are born again we become new creatures in Christ. Paul writes, 'Therefore, if anyone is in Christ, he is a new creation; old things have passed away; behold, all things have become new' (2 Corinthians 5:17).

Our Bible reading tells us of the new character of the Christian. Paul first of all outlines the traits of the godless person. Then he tells us of the ‘fruit of the Spirit’. The first thing mentioned is love. Our text tells us that love is the great mark of the Christian. Now look at your character and ask yourself, ‘Do I really love God and the people of this world? Do I show Christian love to all — not just the people who are my friends, but even to those who I find hard to be friends with?’

Christians are people who dare to be different in this world, because they are members of the kingdom of Jesus Christ. No longer are they citizens of the kingdom of Satan. At times it is hard to be different. But always remember that Christ loved you so much that he willingly came into this world to die in your place upon that dreadful cross. You owe him everything. Now begin to show your thankfulness by being different from the godless people of the world.

Reader, may God bless you greatly and may it be said of you, ‘Look at that person. See the love that is shown to all? That person must be a Christian.’

Activities

1. What did Jesus say was the ‘great commandment’?
2. In what way is a Christian different from other people?
3. Whose kingdom does a Christian belong to?
4. What is meant by Christian ‘love’?

If you have received spiritual blessings from reading this book, please send a postcard of your homeland to:

James A. Cromarty,
3 Appaloosa Place,
Wingham, N.S.W.
Australia 2429.